Ford's Wonderful World *of Golf*

Ford's
Wonderful World
of Golf

Tim Philpot

LINKS PLAYERS PUBLISHING

A ministry of Links Players International

La Quinta, California

FORD'S WONDERFUL WORLD OF GOLF

Copyright © 2013 by Tim Philpot
ISBN 978-0-9831422-2-5

Links Players International is a mission organization committed to seeing people of influence in the kingdom of the world transformed by Jesus Christ that they may become people of impact in the kingdom of God. We normally open contact with people in and around country clubs and golf courses.
Find out more at www.linksplayers.com.

Expanded photographs and author's notes at
www.fordswonderfulworld.com.

- CHAPTERS -

- *PREFACE* -

My father's name was Ford.

Ford Philpot.

He was either a preacher who played golf, or a golfer who preached. Not sure which.

These stories are a tribute to a man who loved God and golf. He found God at age 30. He found golf at age 44.

Perhaps it is better theology to say God found him at age 30. And golf found him at age 44.

He loved both.

Both God and golf "seek and search" for wayward souls. And when they find someone like Ford, it is forever.

Ford died more than 20 years ago. But he has not left.

I am now my father in many ways, especially on the golf course.

Especially when I get tempted to improve a bad lie.

Especially when I tinker with a new putter or driver, hoping the problem is the club and not the man.

Especially when I find myself bragging about a good round—or even just one good shot—and totally ignoring the ones that followed.

Especially when I quit the game, but then find myself playing again the next week.

Ford did his best to teach his sons. He was like all fathers in that no one actually showed him how to do that. His own dad ("PawPaw" to me) was a good man but not much of a teacher about family things.

In hindsight, golf was the stage for many of Ford's lessons about life.

THIS BOOK IS NOT HIS BIOGRAPHY. Such a book already exists. *It Took a Miracle* was written by his friend Herb Bowdoin in 1964 when Ford was only 47. It was a nice book about a famous preacher, but not the whole story. The title almost says it all. In truth, he was a hopeless drunk transformed by God. But like many biographies, this one presented the professional preacher Ford as almost perfect after he met the Lord. Ford's golf buddies knew better.

And of course there was a long way to go when the book was written. Ford still had 27 years and about 3,000 golf games to go.

My story tries to be "the truth, the whole truth and nothing but the truth, so help me God." I hope to draw a more complete picture of how Ford "finished the course," as the Bible says in 2 Timothy 4.

This is also my own story. Many of the stories are my own golf adventures. I am old enough now to realize that Ford's story became my story at some point. I morphed into my father a few years ago after he passed away.

So this is simply a son's version of a good but imperfect father. I am comforted by the fact that he was not that perfect man I thought he was when I was 10 years old. That would have been a lot of pressure to live up to. As I learned over time, he was very human, which makes me feel better about me.

Like a good golf game, he left room for improvement in his sons.

So, here goes. Welcome to Ford's Wonderful World of Golf.

— *Tim Philpot, September 22, 2012*

- SUDDEN DEATH -

MOUNTAIN MAN

*"Whoever touches
the mountain is to be
put to death."*
Exodus 19:12

F ORD NEVER TOUCHED A CLUB UNTIL 1961, when he was 44 years old. He grew up in the mountains of Kentucky, where golf was not a real sport.

Ford was from Clay County, deep in those mountains, where feuds were serious business.

On July 18, 1899, the feud in Clay County involving the Philpots was front page news in *The New York Times*.

All the Philpots were sided with the Bakers.

The Whites and Howards and Griffins and Benges comprised the enemy.

In the context of golf, I suppose I should like Ian Baker-Finch. Who knows? If he's partly a Baker, he can't be all bad.

I cannot pull for the Los Angeles Lakers as long as Dwight Howard plays center for them.

Or the Clippers, if Blake Griffin is their power forward. Reggie White was supposed to be a really good man. Not sure on that, though.

That's just how it is for us Philpots. Anyone from the

Whites and Griffins and Howards is suspect at best.

The blood was so bad between the Philpots and these other families that when a Philpot was sent to prison for murder, one of the others committed a crime just so he could also go to prison in hopes of getting his revenge on Jim Philpot.

Consider the following from a front page *New York Times* article from the 1890s about Clay County:

> *To give still greater strength to the brothers of "Tom" Baker, the powerful Philpot family is beginning to take sides against the Whites and Howards.*
>
> *The Philpots and Whites, while Republicans, belong to separate factions, and the Philpots have been on the "outs"... for so long a time that there is much feeling between the followers of the two families.*
>
> *In one voting precinct in this county, every voter is either a Philpot or kin to one.*
>
> *They are rich, and at the same time desperate men, having been engaged in numerous pistol and rifle battles.*
>
> *It is said of the Philpots that no man ever shot at one of them and lived to die a natural death if he remained in Clay County.*

So, Ford Philpot's people are, among other things:

1. on the 'outs'
2. rich
3. desperate
4. friends of anyone named Baker
5. enemies of anyone named White, Howard, or Griffin
6. Republicans
7. and gun owners.

And don't forget my personal favorite: if anyone shoots at a Philpot, we cannot let that person die a natural death.

Sudden death takes on a whole new meaning if you ever find yourself tied at the end of 72 holes with a Philpot.

Knowing me and my family well, the modern day Philpots have other traits:

1. we get the shanks and yips on occasion
2. we three-putt too often
3. we love Arnold Palmer and Raymond Floyd
4. and we love to hit the ball right to left.

These ancestors may help you understand why Ford Philpot did not like to lose on the golf course.

Ford was a mountain man.

2

- *'YES, GOLF IS A SPORT'* -

SPORTS FAN

*Anyone who competes
as an athlete...*
2 Timothy 2:5

IN THE HILLS OF KENTUCKY, all that mattered was round-ball, known now as basketball. Ford was a star at Manchester High School. They often practiced on dirt patches outdoors. Makes you wonder if they threw up grass to check the wind like golfers do. The gym was pitiful. It was 1935.

Ford got mad that spring, quit school without graduating, and literally ran away to Hamilton, Ohio. Thanks to basketball, he got a job with the Ford Motor Company, playing on their semi-professional team, which was an odd and poor precursor to the current professional basketball leagues. So in the middle of the Depression, Ford had work. He was 18.

He later stayed connected to the game as a referee. After he moved to Wilmore, Kentucky, in 1947 to start college as a 30-year-old freshman, he found himself helping famous coach Adolph Rupp by refereeing many practices. Knowing Ford, I am sure he just walked in one day to Coach Rupp's office and told the famous coach who he was and how he'd like to referee practice. And Coach Rupp said, "Sure."

Ford loved sports of all kinds. The Cincinnati Reds were a passion, especially after he met and drank with some of the players from 1935 to 1942, while working in various restaurants in downtown Cincinnati. He always acted like he knew Johnny Vander Meer, who pitched two straight no-hitters. Turns out he did. I finally met Vander Meer when Ford and Johnny were both way over the hill.

One of my primary childhood memories of revival-preaching Dad is vivid. Virtually every night he was out of town. The preaching service would end around 9 PM or so. He would be in his car by 9:30. If it was summer, the radio dial was tuned to WLW in Cincinnati, the famous 50,000-watt station where the Cincinnati Reds presided over the airwaves. If he was in Florida or Georgia, the radio crackled and popped through static as Ford tried to hear enough to know if the Reds won or lost. Waite Hoyt was the announcer. The former Yankee pitcher was now an odd storytelling radio man.

To this day, just like Ford, I always feel better if the Reds have won, even if they are 16½ games out of first place in September. And I am slightly depressed when they lose, even if they were mathematically eliminated last week.

If it was winter, the same radio would be looking for Louisville's WHAS to catch the Kentucky Wildcats. If the radio did not provide information and the game was still going, Ford would call home and tell my mother, Ginny, to put the radio up to the phone. He needed to know. He needed to know if they won. He needed the score. He was a fan. He could have bought season tickets for what the phone call cost.

Basketball was a real sport for sure. Baseball too.

But golf? Is it a sport? In the 1930s, Ford would have said an emphatic, "No!" It was just a game of some sort. Like pool. Probably good for gambling but not a real sport. Only rich people played the game as far as he could tell.

And when golf first came on the scene with Arnold Palmer and Gary Player and Jack Nicklaus in the late 1950s, most great golfers could be seen playing with a cigarette hanging out of their mouths.

It is surely an enduring image of Arnie, squinting into the sun with a cigarette hanging from his lip, flicking it away so he could hit the shot, then picking the smoke up again off the fairway grass in time to take a puff and walk to the green, cigarette in hand. Hogan did the same. Even Nicklaus smoked in the beginning.

The old TV show *Celebrity Golf*, hosted by Arnold himself, almost always showed Arnie and his guest, someone like Perry Como or Bob Hope, smoking cigarettes while they played this so-called "sport."

Can you imagine Kobe Bryant going to the bench for a puff on his Marlboro to relax during a television timeout?

Or Peyton Manning drawing deep while the defense is on the field?

Yet even today, John Daly can be caught sneaking some puffs when he thinks the cameras are not around.

But no matter whether golf is a mere game or a real sport, it got the attention of Ford Philpot in 1961. He was 44 years old and had no idea how the game itself would redefine the next 30 years of his life.

3

PICADOME

"Rejoice with me;
I have found my lost coin."
Luke 15:9

Gay Brewer, known as "Junior" to his friends, grew up at Picadome Golf Course, a simple public course in the middle of Lexington, Kentucky. In fact, the course is now named after him. Gay put Lexington on the golf map when he got to the PGA Tour, and even won the Masters. My first memory on a golf course with Dad was at Picadome.

It was 1961. I was ten years old. Arnold Palmer was a big deal. People like Billy Casper, Ben Hogan, Dow Finsterwald and Art Wall were names I had heard. Julius Boros seemed cool. Jack Nicklaus was some young kid and still an amateur.

Picadome had an unusual start because the first two holes were par-5s. Hole number one goes straight out and the second green sits next to the first tee, stretching straight back to the clubhouse.

A good player always had a chance to be two strokes under after two holes, which was nice. Also, it was a good place to quit after two holes and go straight to the bar if a bad day had already started. You could even start all over again and pretend like the first two holes were just warm-up.

My first golf memory was traumatic. My current golf nightmares may be explained by that first day on the course.

Ford was playing the first hole at Picadome. I have no recollection of who his companions were that day. I was following, probably just riding along in a golf cart, acting like a caddie. Like post-traumatic stress disorder soldiers, I just don't remember exactly what happened next.

NEAR A CREEK ON THE RIGHT that separated the first and second holes was a Wilson golf ball that seemed to belong to nobody. What a treasure I had found! I was totally unaware that coming down the second fairway was some old slicer whose ball was hit to the right, as usual. He was looking for his ball.

He thought it was lost. Actually, it was not lost. It was in my pocket.

In a fit of conscience that I regret to this day, I confessed that I had picked up the ball. I got my first lesson in golf etiquette.

Did that old slicer call me a stupid kid or did I just remember it that way? Who knows, but to this day, I don't pick up balls quickly.

But that day, golf hooked me.

What was it?

The sight of the ball going out of sight?

Or the sound of a ball going in the cup?

Or just wanting to be like Dad, or at least be with him?

Who knows, but I was hooked. I liked everything about it. It seemed like a chance for someone like me with limited athletic ability to beat someone.

I was slow. I was weak.

But golf fit my personality immediately.

Especially great for kids like me who like to shoot every time they touch the ball.

No need to pass to a teammate.

Just me and the ball. Great game.

4

WIFFLE BALL

Teach them to your children,
talking about them
when you sit at home.
Deuteronomy 11:19

FORD AND I WERE LEARNING GOLF at about the same time. He was 44 and I was 10.

Ford didn't know there was such a thing as a country club to join. He eventually joined Tates Creek in about 1964, a short but nice hilly course.

But in the beginning I was left to try to learn golf by myself in my backyard. Ford was a travelling preacher and therefore not available much.

I first learned how hard it is to hit a ball straight playing with a golf Wiffle ball around my house in Lexington, Kentucky.

Jack Nicklaus learned to play at the famous Scioto Country Club under the tutelage of professional Jack Grout.

Bobby Jones learned to play at East Lake Golf Club in Atlanta under the care of famous Scottish pro Stewart Maiden. He imitated the old pro and became a legend.

I learned to play at 171 Edgemoor Drive under the seldom watchful eye of Ford Philpot.

No wonder I'm no good.

OUR FAMILY LIVED A *LEAVE IT TO BEAVER* EXISTENCE. My mother, Virginia, was a soccer mom before anyone played soccer. She took my younger brother Danny and me to every game and practice for every sport we played, which was everything. Danny and I both played on the Saints in Little League baseball, so named because Ford's religious TV show *The Story* was our sponsor.

Danny went on to be a good football player, but I was too weak and too slow.

Slow and weak is a bad combination for all real sports. But not for golf.

Our house sat in a simple neighborhood in middle class America. The backyard was big enough to play some football. We had a basketball goal where I shot free throws, even in the snow. I learned too late that being a good free throw shooter doesn't actually help if you are too slow and too weak to draw fouls.

And we had a great fence to hit homeruns in Wiffle ball baseball.

We had a dog named Lady who was my best friend. She was a bird dog with papers, who we completely and sadly domesticated. She had several litters of puppies by way of the collie up the street. She had the cutest pups because they were all different. Some had long hair and looked like collies and some looked like Lady, a short-haired pointer. I now realize that Lady was more a "woman of the world" than a real lady, presenting herself to the collie annually. But some of my best childhood memories are sleeping in the doghouse with Lady and her odd assortment of puppies named by Danny and me.

After Lady had gone to doggie heaven, we found Tao. Everyone hated Tao except our family. He was a miniature fox terrier. He barked a lot and bit people on occasion. Tao would actually hike his leg on you if given the opportunity.

Ford claimed to hate little house dogs, which is the normal position of any real mountain man, but the new puppy Tao licked him and suddenly Tao became the new man of the house in charge of everything.

Tao was a disaster but he loved his family, which was the Philpots. If he had not been my dog, I would have hated Tao.

We even had a pet squirrel at one time. My mom found a nearly dead baby squirrel in the yard and saved him. She nursed him back to health. He stayed in a cage, and then we trusted him to live in the woodpile on the back porch at night and roam our house at day. He was even in one of our Christmas pictures (Ford, Virginia, Tim, Danny, Tao and "Feo" the squirrel, all gathered in front of the fireplace).

Feo was sitting on my shoulder, and I thought it was normal. No wonder I need therapy.

IN THE MIDST OF THIS 1950S SITCOM CHILDHOOD was the golf course I set up around our house.

I don't remember the holes very well. There were doglegs around the corner of the house. Lots of bushes. Out of bounds in the street. On top of the house was also OB. No relief from Lady's doghouse. No replays if the ball hit the telephone wires. Play it as it lies, sort of. Replace all divots, since Mom did not appreciate holes in her yard.

Wiffle balls curve a lot. It was easy to hit slices and hooks. For me, it is still easy to hit slices and hooks. Just don't ask me to hit it straight.

I also learned that the ball went best when you swung easy. I still find that true.

Closely related to the Wiffle ball course was the putting course inside the house. Many a contest was played between the Pro Special ball, the Hogan ball, the Wilson ball, the Maxfli ball, the Titleist ball or whatever was available. The Spalding Dot was much coveted.

I would not only play the game but also commentate. I was Chris Schenkel or Curt Gowdy, whispering: "The Maxfli really needs this one. He's one down with two to play."

Most exciting though was the Dunlop "small ball" played in the British Isles. Or a Slazenger.

Somehow, Ford always had some of those around. He thought a small ball went farther and was easier to get into the hole, so he conspired to have some around. He was into technology way before its time.

My lonely contest usually wandered up and down the hallway outside my bedroom, played to the "pin" that was a leg of the couch in the living room.

Perhaps in hindsight this was all a bad idea. Think about it. I hit thousands of putts and none of them ever went into a hole. I got accustomed to the ball staying up. Not a good idea maybe.

5

- 'I THINK IT WENT IN!' -
MASON HEADLEY

So Jacob was left alone.
Genesis 32:24

ACROSS THE STREET FROM PICADOME was a young golfer's paradise. It was a driving range, a putt-putt course with real holes, and an 18-hole, par-3 course that could be played all day for almost nothing. It was even lighted for night play. It was on Mason Headley Road. If it had a name, it is forgotten.

Ford was typically gone three out of four weeks preaching, so my golf was mostly to be learned without his assistance, which may have been good, in hindsight.

My mother dropped me off many summer mornings, starting in probably 1962. It is all a blur now, but here is what I think I remember.

The driving range had "metal" woods. They were considered inferior. No one even dreamed of using one on a real course.

They had hot dogs inside. You could play 72 holes or more in a day with no problem for the same price, probably $1.50. The price included rental clubs, which were odd-numbered irons. Putter, 3-iron, 5-iron, 7-iron, 9-iron and wedge.

The tees were rubber mats. And there was some sort of

Astroturf type carpet for those who did not like the rubber tee stuck in concrete.

You could play by yourself, which I liked. I must have been a loner.

I MADE A HOLE-IN-ONE THE FIRST YEAR I PLAYED. It was a 3-iron from about 105. I seem to remember it was the second hole, but it was likely my 38th hole of the day.

I was playing by myself. I thought to myself: *I think it went in!* It did.

The sight of a golf ball disappearing is, to this day, one of God's rare beauties.

No one attested it, so… was it really a hole-in-one? Ask a purist. If a tree falls in the woods and no one hears it…?

Actually, to be fair, some old man saw it happen, just like in a TV commercial. I was definitely hooked.

Baseball grip. No golf gloves. No lessons or technique. Just get it in the hole as soon as possible. Great game for a weak white kid with fair hand-eye coordination but otherwise limited athletic ability.

I also remember very well sitting on a bench behind the eleventh tee when a ball long and right off number ten hit me square in the back of the head and knocked me out cold for a few moments. Golf is not for sissies.

My mother wondered how you can get hurt playing golf. I tried to explain it, but I don't think she heard me. I was not a lawyer yet, so I didn't know you could sue people for stuff like that.

I was happy just being on the course. I had found a home.

6

WILMORE
*"You who call yourselves
citizens of the holy city."*
Isaiah 48:2

FORD LOVED EASY GOLF COURSES. Perhaps that all started at Wilmore, a small college town just 15 miles from Lexington, affectionately referred to as "the Holy City" by those who knew the place. We actually lived there until 1959. Wilmore is dominated by Asbury College and Seminary and thus the "holy city" reference. I went to first and second grade there and it was definitely more "Christian" than any so-called Christian school could ever be. And they had a golf course.

This is where I graduated from par-3 golf and played real golf with Ford on a real course. I do not precisely remember the first time.

I do know it was on Wilmore's nine-hole, Bermuda grass course built by people who obviously did not play golf. Bermuda greens in central Kentucky were unheard of. It is a stretch to call Wilmore a real course.

But I did learn there that Bermuda grass has grain.

The term "goat ranch" has been loosely used by some, but I would not call Wilmore such a thing, because I would not want to denigrate goats or those who ranch them. It was owned by Asbury College, where not a single soul knew one thing about the game of golf.

The "clubhouse" was a small cement-block building, which must have been built more for use as a storage unit.

There was definitely no bar and no nice looking pink or yellow golf clothes for sale. No shoes either. Maybe some hotdogs. But none of that mattered. It was real golf.

"Old man Layborn" gave you a scorecard and a pencil and some encouragement to go have a nice day.

Somehow I still get a thrill just thinking about being in their pitiful pro shop (with no pro) and getting permission to step to the first tee.

INITIALLY WE PLAYED A LOT WITH SERGIUS LEACH, one of my dad's friends who very reluctantly allowed Ford's kid to play with them. He was a nervous sort. He had been the best tennis player in Kentucky when he was young and was now a mediocre golfer. He hated mediocre, but that is what he was. He taught me not to stand behind anyone making a golf swing. Or make noise. Or move a muscle.

So, Serge helped me learn some golf etiquette with his wave of the hand and evil eye when I was standing in the wrong place. He actually hit bad drives because of me, or so he thought. It had nothing to do with his four-piece swing and old age.

We also played with Lee Fisher, a psychology professor at Asbury College who first taught me about how to "psych out" an opponent. He was a really bad golfer, so defense was his only chance.

And then we played with Charlie Crouse, who was one of Dad's best friends and also a really poor player. Memories of Charlie's swing haunt me to this day. He never stopped moving, like a piece of rope with a stick on the end. He was a tall man who could hit it long when all the pieces fell together just right, which was about once a day. Charlie's local claim to fame was that he owned the local graveyard. I'm still not sure how one acquires a graveyard, but Charlie was present for every funeral at Wilmore Graveyard to protect his investment.

The saying is that taxes and death are the two things that cannot be avoided. In Wilmore, that list also included bad lies and Charlie Crouse.

FORD HIMSELF WAS ONE OF THOSE GOOD ATHLETES who was finding out that being fast once upon a time, or good at shooting hoops, or a pool shark, was not necessarily a help in golf. But he also saw that golf was a beautiful game for someone in their 40s who loved to compete.

He was hooked.

The first hole at Wilmore was a par-3 of about 150 yards. The ninth hole was a dogleg-right, 460-yard par-5 that went around a track and soccer field. The scorecard actually stated that it was illegal to hit the ball over the soccer field, even though a decent drive left a simple shot over the field to the ninth green. No one obeyed the rule.

The course was, in hindsight, a joke. But I loved it.

I have now travelled to more than 80 countries in world and played golf in half of them. I have been to Scotland and Ireland numerous times. I have played at many famous and wonderful clubs.

But I have never enjoyed any golf game like I did at Wilmore.

THERE WERE A LOT OF "FIRSTS" AT WILMORE. I recall when I was able to hit it over the water for the first time on the fourth hole, a short par-4. I had my first real birdie. And it was there that I broke 80 for the first time.

I am sure Ford loved Wilmore simply because he was a serious threat to break 80 every day.

7

- 'I SEE THAT HAND!' -

CAMP MEETING

Abraham built an altar there...
He bound his son Isaac
and laid him on the altar.
Genesis 22:9

A LONG WITH BEING THE HOME OF ASBURY COLLEGE and Asbury Seminary, Wilmore also hosted a camp meeting every summer.

Ford was a camp meeting preacher. He was often invited to preach at the Wilmore Camp Meeting, a two-week affair every July. Kentucky in July is hot and steamy.

He preached services at 10 AM, 2:30 PM, and 7:30 PM. Everyone attended in the morning and evening. The 2:30 meeting was only for serious and holy people—or that was how it seemed.

One of my distinct memories of my camp meeting childhood is a thought that there are two of everything. Maybe this comes somehow from the story of Noah and the ark, where two of every animal went on the boat.

I knew there was male and female, but I also soon realized there were Republicans and Democrats. There were Protestants and Catholics. The movies had good guys and bad guys. Roy Rogers wore a white hat. The bad guys always wore black hats. Life was simple and understandable.

And in the case of preachers, there were also two kinds.

Notice that I say "preachers." Ford was not really a minister. Certainly not a pastor. Barely a "reverend." He was a preacher. There is a difference.

And there were two kinds of preachers: Those who would sweat and those who did not sweat.

My pastor at the Methodist church was Donald Durham. He was the kind who did not sweat (and therefore barely worth listening to). I now realize he was a really good man and fine preacher.

But my dad was a preacher who would sweat (and therefore worth listening to).

He would preach so hard that he would end up wet. A sermon was not a 25-minute talk. It was a 60-minute, sweat-filled, tear-jerking, voice-challenging halftime speech by a great football coach, urging the team/congregation not to let this opportunity for heaven slip by. These meetings would be conducted in small country churches in the 1950s. Later, they moved under the big tent after Ford got the outdoor tabernacle that became one of his trademarks. No air conditioning. Lots of funeral parlor fans waving to keep cool. As it got dark by the end of the service, even the fireflies (lightning bugs to some) seemed interested in what was happening under the tent. The "revival" was often the biggest thing happening in town, and Ford's preaching was the main attraction.

But my greatest memory of Ford was not really his preaching. It came from his time at that altar, praying with people for perhaps another hour, "praying through" until the victory was won. The invitation to come to Jesus was always there. Many nights I recall the last ones to leave were the sweating preacher and a repentant sinner made new.

Camp meeting was a place where a lot of that happened.

The sermon was preached. Then "all eyes closed and raise your hand if God is speaking to you."

"I see that hand." And then for some, "Come to the altar. Don't wait. Come now."

The afternoon services were for the pious and sanctified folks. My youthful perception was that these older saints existed to lay a guilt trip on everyone else—that is, everyone who was not interested in wearing a coat and tie and sitting through "church" from 2:30 to 4:00 on a July afternoon when it was 93 degrees.

No one but children and unserious Christians would go play games during camp meeting.

I was both. So playing golf in Wilmore during camp meeting was especially exciting, because it made you feel like a real sinner.

The only way to get onto the course was to skip the afternoon services and even the supposedly fun activities they arranged for the kids, like softball. (Swimming was *not* available, since some saw bathing suits as another form of sin.) The list of available fun activities was pretty small at camp meeting. Golf was not on the list.

So I loved to go play golf during camp meeting. I was, in theory, supposed to be back at the camp, preferably even at the altar, seeking forgiveness for my many sins. Instead, I was committing another one by sneaking off to play golf. It felt so right.

8

- 'GUYS, DON'T FORGET ME!' -

SAVING SOULS

*They reel to and fro, and
stagger like a drunken man,
and are at their wit's end.*
Psalm 107:27

FORD GOT SO HOOKED ON GOLF that when someone would ask him how the latest revival meeting went he would say, "Not too good. I couldn't make a putt."

He was only half kidding.

And I noticed he preached a lot in Florida in the winter when you couldn't play golf in Kentucky. Maybe sinners go south in the winter? Golfers do.

I think he was even sneaking off during camp meetings on hot July afternoons to play golf at Wilmore when he was supposed to be on the platform listening to one of the other preachers explain John Wesley's theology of entire sanctification.

But it is true that he actually may have produced more souls for the Kingdom of Heaven on the golf course than at the church or local tent revival.

He had been a terrible alcoholic until age 30.

He then met Jesus. The biography about Dad's life was called *It Took a Miracle*. And it did.

For him, it was October 1947. He entered Asbury College as a 30-year-old freshman. Since he did not graduate high school, he entered on probation, hoping his experience of 37 months in the Marines and 12 years in the workforce would qualify him to do college work.

A few fellow students invited Ford to a "prayer meeting," presuming he was a preacher boy. They were unaware that Ford was a drunk, still sneaking off to Lexington to local bars. But this was his moment. He confessed, "Guys, while you pray, don't forget me." And he confessed his sins and found Jesus dramatically around midnight.

The same absurd passion for alcohol was turned into saving souls. He went to class the next day and was asked by a fellow student if he was a preacher. He said, "Yes," although he had been a follower of Jesus for only eight hours!

And then, 14 years later, at age 44, he added a passion for golf to his passion for God.

If he met anyone on the local golf course, they would soon learn that he was in town to preach and they should come on down and hear him at the local church or tent or gymnasium or football stadium. Many stories of men met on a golf course became stories of sinners redeemed.

He was a Marine, too, so the combination of Marine, golfer and sports fan made him seem fantastic to every man he met. He had lots of fans.

Especially me.

9

- 'RIGHT EDGE, BWANA' -
CONGO GOLF

*All the ends of the earth
will remember and
turn to the LORD.*
Psalm 22:27

F ORD WAS A PRETTY BIG-TIME EVANGELIST before the very
word "evangelist" became a dirty word.

He arguably preached to more people in the 1960s than
anyone except Billy Graham himself, especially if you count
television, since Ford's program *The Story* was the first
religious color TV show in America. The first show aired in
1959, and he was seen by five million people every week in
his prime.

Millions of people knew his name. He liked being
famous. And I thought it was pretty cool at the time. Only in
adulthood and after the scandals of TV preachers did I ever
have a negative thought about Ford and television.

He preached in Africa a few times, to as many as 100,000
people.

But even then he was always wondering if they had a golf
course. In Kinshasha, Congo, in 1966, he found such a place.
I was 15 and went with him on this African adventure.

I remember dirt greens, people wandering all over the

course, and women walking with buckets of water balanced on their heads while we tried to hit an old 2-wood off a crooked tee box. We had so many caddies they were fighting over who would get to carry my pitiful old rental clubs. The expert caddies were interesting: "Right edge, Bwana," they would say. On a dirt green. Not much grain.

Preach at night and play during the day. That was Ford's style. It worked in small town America. It worked in big cities. It worked in Africa.

10

- 'LOVE, PHIL' -

GINNY

*He who finds a wife finds
what is good and receives
favor from the LORD.*
Proverbs 18:22

N O DISCUSSION OF FORD should be undertaken without a chapter on "Ginny."

In 1939, Virginia Robinson was a beautiful and smart 25-year-old girl living near Cincinnati, Ohio. She was the second of eight children. She had been a straight-A high school student who started college in 1931 at age 17.

But as Virginia's adult life was getting started, so was the Great Depression. For her, it became very personal when her father Burns was caught stealing on the mail train where he worked. Burns went to prison. He was a good man who stole to support his Depression Era family, or at least that is the story our family now tells. He got caught.

So, the older kids had to chip in and help put food on the table for the younger ones. Virginia was brought home from college and became a secretary for a lawyer.

By 1939 she was the secretary for John Lair, a famous musician who was known throughout the country as the founder of the Renfro Valley Barn Dance, a Saturday night radio event heard by millions on the 100,000-watt Cincinnati station WLW.

Lair then decided to move his Cincinnati-based operation back to his home place in the foothills of the Kentucky mountains. He built Renfro Valley to be the home of country music.

It never really happened. Opryland got that honor. But Renfro Valley was the Opryland of the world in 1939.

Virginia followed Mr. Lair to live and work in Rockcastle County, Kentucky.

Renfro Valley was hiring people to do everything. They needed someone to run their restaurant. A cocky young kid named Ford Philpot was 22 when he waltzed into the Cincinnati office for an interview. He had experience in the bars and restaurants of Cincinnati hotels and was a hillbilly himself.

Ford was hired. He became a one-man show in the restaurant. He would take the orders, shout back into the kitchen ("two eggs over easy"), then run back into the kitchen and cook breakfast. He knew how to make it look like a big operation. Those skills came in handy down the road.

But the real find of 1939 at Renfro Valley was Virginia, soon to be known as Ginny.

They married on July 24, 1940. A honeymoon followed to visit Ford's relatives in Arkansas.

Yes, you might be a redneck if you go visit relatives in Arkansas for your honeymoon.

You would think that Ginny, being a 4.0 GPA sort of person, would have gotten the clue that Ford was not exactly a great candidate for marriage.

But apparently she loved him. Everybody loved Ford.

IN 1940, HE WAS FUNNY. He looked good with no shirt. He

could cook. He drank, but not too much. He didn't waste time playing golf. He had a car. But most importantly he was passionate about his love for Ginny.

When Ginny met Ford, everyone was calling him "Phil," so she did too. So as long as I remember, my father was Phil to my mom.

He even signed his letters "Love, Phil." Her letters began, "Dear Phil."

Ford and Virginia were Phil and Ginny to each other.

If I know anything for sure, it is that love and marriage keep the world sane.

Lovers like Phil and Ginny produce children who know they are on the earth because of love, not some random act. The greatest gift my parents ever gave me was their love for each other.

We are losing that concept now in the Western world and my heart gets heavy on occasion about it all.

Thanks, Ginny. Thanks for not leaving Ford when your family said, "Leave him. He's a drunk."

Thanks for loving God enough to give a wayward man a "mulligan." He needed it. I was born four years later. Yes, Ginny gave Ford a mulligan, which means that my first second chance came several years before I was even born!

This is probably just one man's version of a story we all could tell. We all get mulligans that are known only in eternity.

11

- FRIED CHICKEN -

COLONEL SANDERS

*He holds success
in store for the upright.*
Proverbs 2:7

RENFRO VALLEY WAS ONLY 20 MILES UP THE ROAD from a gas station and restaurant in Corbin, Kentucky, operated by Harland Sanders, an odd man who wore a white suit at times and claimed to have the best chicken in the world. In 1939, Harland was 49 years old and only mildly successful.

He actually was an aspiring politician. He later ran for State Senate in 1951 and lost in a Republican primary. He must have forgotten that he could have put a "chicken in every pot."

But at age 61, it appeared that Harland Sanders was a mediocre success, at best, as a chicken entrepreneur and a dismal failure, at worst, as a politician.

Losing a Republican primary in Kentucky is one of the surest signs of failure known to man.

The Colonel got back on track after losing the election and continued to fry chicken until he finally became known in the 1960s as the famous Colonel Sanders, well after his 70th birthday.

No one has any clue what his claim was to be called a

Colonel. I guess you can call yourself anything you want, which may explain "Reverend" Al Sharpton. In fact, colonels are as common in Kentucky as crows.

Anyway, Ford became dear friends with Harland Sanders in about 1939, a relationship that was one of his proudest connections. He was glad to be able to say to people that Colonel Sanders was his buddy.

An interview with the Colonel on TV was one of Ford's high moments. They discussed the old days and how both of them had come from "nothing" to "something." Ford and the Colonel were both perfect examples of God's grace. Mulligans abound. It's never too late to start over. It's never too late to open your eyes to the possibilities of success.

12

NO STRANGERS

*"For I was a stranger
and you invited me in."*
Matthew 25:35

F ORD NEVER MET A STRANGER. That was especially helpful in 1969 when I went with him to my first PGA event at the NCR Club in Dayton, Ohio.

Unlike some of my early fuzzy memories of golf with Ford, I remember that Friday so well.

It was the first time I physically laid eyes on Jack Nicklaus and Gary Player and Arnold Palmer. That is not something you forget if you are a golfer.

At the risk of being accused of being sacrilegious, seeing the "Big Three" in person was almost like the first day in heaven with the Holy Trinity. I was breathless.

Jack Nicklaus was bigger than life to me. I saw him coming down the ninth fairway. He was actually much blonder than I thought, and also not a real bear. Who knows what I was looking for, but I was impressed that he was a real person, only about 5 feet, 10 inches tall.

I recall that he actually looked at me once. I felt like Moses on the mountain with the eyes of God Himself on me. I turned my face because the awesomeness of Jack Nicklaus staring at me was more than I could handle.

It was probably my imagination, but I remember it so well.

Gary Player was also amazing to see. All black clothes in the heat of August. He was, of course, from South Africa, and protestors had vandalized a green to support their black brothers who were suffering from apartheid. I remember that Ford commented that he did not see "how pouring gas on a green in Dayton, Ohio, could help Nelson Mandela sitting in a jail in Africa, but who knows, maybe they were right."

I do know that Gary Player was not the problem. He was a gentleman and part of the answer.

BUT ARNOLD PALMER WAS A TOTALLY DIFFERENT EXPERIENCE. He had shot 80 or so the first day and only went to the course on that Friday to withdraw due to some ailment (probably bad putting). He was literally leaving the property, in the parking lot, when we walked up that morning.

I recall punching my father and saying, "Dad, look, that's *Arnold Palmer.*" And it was.

He was walking to a car where his clubs were being loaded for a quiet exit.

Dad walked straight up to him, stuck out his hand, and said, "Hello Arnie. I'm Ford Philpot."

Arnie was as polite and nice as you would hope or imagine. Within 60 seconds, Ford told him about a course he and friends were building in Florida. Maybe Arnie should come down and check it out.

He then proceeded to lie to Arnie about how good his son Tim played golf. He introduced me as if I would be on tour soon. The facts were that Tim had been mostly the fourth or fifth man on a high school golf team. But to hear Ford talk, his son was a highly recruited prodigy.

I thought I would die.

But in fact, Dad's words, though painfully false, caused me to want to be as good as he said.

I never made it, but I haven't quit trying to make him proud.

This was one of my dad's forgivable sins.

He later told someone I had won a tournament that I had not even played in.

Why did he tell such lies? Not sure.

But he loved to believe that his kids were something special. That put pressure on my brother and me to make it happen. Not healthy, but true.

13

LOOKING GOOD

*In all Israel there was not
a man so highly praised for
his handsome appearance.*
2 Samuel 14:25

FORD LIKED TO LOOK GOOD. Pictures of him, even as a boy, show a cocky little guy who liked to have his picture taken.

Thus golf was perfect for him.

Football was not a good fit because the helmet and uniform meant that no one could see the player.

Basketball was a better fit for him, since you were seen, even in short shorts.

He liked to be seen, which may explain his desire to be a preacher and, even more, a TV preacher.

He had played semi-professional basketball in Cincinnati in the 1930s. The shorts were really short back then and he loved his legs. So did girls, I suspect.

But golf was perfect.

One of the beauties of golf is the ability to turn it into a fashion show. Golf history is full of pretty boys wearing purple or some other color no man in his right mind would wear on the street.

Doug Sanders comes to mind. Payne Stewart's knickers gave him a reputation.

In the modern era, Ian Poulter and Rickie Fowler are obviously not afraid of attention.

Way back, even Walter Hagen was right spiffy. The old boys would never play golf without a coat and tie.

Bobby Jones looked great in a long-sleeved white shirt and tie when it was over 100 degrees in Minneapolis as he won the 1930 U.S. Open.

So golf gave Dad the opportunity to wear yellow pants without being called a sissy.

Even pink is OK in a clubhouse or pro shop. Shoes with tassels. Shoes with white and brown to match a brown outfit.

And being outdoors gave him reason to work on his tan. He sure was not going to get it working in the yard. I do not remember even one second when Ford did work in the yard. Mow the grass? Are you serious? "I'm too busy preaching and playing golf." Ginny took care of the grass.

As he got older, however, he forgot that plaid pants and paisley shirts didn't look good together. He may have been color blind too. But good for him, he didn't care. If he thought he looked good, he looked good.

The opinion of others was not big on his list. His opinion was what mattered most.

14

- 'WANNA PLAY?' -

PRACTICE

*"But do not do what they do,
for they do not practice
what they preach."*

Matthew 23:3

I NEVER RECALL, NOT EVEN ONCE, seeing Ford practice the game of golf. He might on rare occasion hit some warm-up balls. But practice? No way.

Golf was a game to be played, not practiced.

He would call me when I had become a young lawyer and simply say: "Tim, wanna play today?" We both knew what play meant. It was not cards. It was not tennis.

The word was unspoken. Golf.

Without knowing it, such an attitude infected me. I never practiced as a kid. I had no lessons until I was a grown man.

Dad just played. So did I. For me, it was 36 holes a day when possible. Morning 18. Lunch consisting of a burger and Coke. Afternoon 18.

Life was about as good as it ever gets at age 14 at Tates Creek Country Club, which had no practice range. Tates Creek was about playing. It was about the game itself, feeling your way to the hole 18 times. It was not about building a pretty swing on a range.

It was about getting from here to there. I loved it.

Humzey Yessin was the pro at Tates Creek. I recall how shocked Humzey was when he heard that I shot a 76 in some little club event. He looked at me as if I must have cheated.

Who knows? Maybe I did.

But Humzey could also get tough, especially on punks like me. I was driving a cart one day and got somewhere near some flowers, and Humzey started screaming at me to be careful. He did not know that Ford was within earshot.

The next thing I knew Humzey and Ford were almost in a fistfight over how to handle this kid. In hindsight, I am sure that Humzey was right. I was being like my dad, ignoring whatever cart signs existed.

In hindsight, I am almost glad that Tates Creek had no place to hit balls. Golf is a game to play, not practice, and I learned that at Tates Creek.

15

- 'HERE, HIT THIS CLUB' -

NEW CLUBS

*Every stroke the LORD lays on
them with his punishing club
will be to the music of timbrels.*
Isaiah 30:32

ALTHOUGH NOT A BELIEVER IN PRACTICE, Ford did always believe in the power of new clubs. He was confident that his game would improve with new and different clubs.

For Ford, instead of practice, the way to get better was to be on the front edge of all technology's improvements.

Ford was playing a titanium shaft driver at least 20 years before anyone thought it was a good idea. It was light. He loved his titanium driver. He especially loved that no one else he knew had one.

Every good drive deserved a comment: "Look at that," with a silly little grin.

Often he wanted you to try it: "Here, hit this club." Sort of like drug dealers who tell little kids: "Try this little boy. You'll like it."

If Arnold Palmer used a putter on a weekend to win a tournament, Ford might be playing the same putter the next week. Even better was a putter no one had ever seen. He loved to be unique and that included his clubs.

He liked Wilson clubs, for some unknown reason. That cursed me with the same inexplicable desire to play Wilson clubs.

He also had some source to get contraband British balls. They were smaller than normal. He was sure they gave him some sort of edge. They go farther maybe.

And whenever he bought them, since they were supposed to be illegal in the U.S.A., he was likely reminded of the excitement of finding beer in Prohibition days.

Anything illegal must surely be illegal for a reason and thus an advantage if you can find it.

I even found myself at one time playing orange golf balls, hoping it would help the yips. And it did. In 1983 I was literally the only person in the British Amateur playing an orange ball. Something about the color triggered a freedom in my brain that said the object was not a ball to be feared. The white ball had become an object of dread and loathing.

Does the hole get bigger if the ball is smaller? Ford thought so.

Does the ball go straighter if the ball is oranger? I thought so.

16

- FIVE PLUS TWO EQUALS SIX -

SINNER

*All have sinned and fall
short of the glory of God.*
Romans 3:23

I KNEW THAT FORD, although a preacher (and a great one), was a sinner not because of Romans 3:23 ("all have sinned and fall short of the glory of God"), but because he was known to "cheat."

I saw him kick it in the rough.

I saw him mark his ball not exactly perfect.

I saw him write down a six when I could have sworn five plus a ball out of bounds was a seven.

I saw him tap down spike marks (younger people don't even know what I mean by spike marks).

I saw him find balls that could not be found: "Here it is. Must have got a good kick." He was a true evangelist, I guess, finding lost Maxflis and saving their souls.

Golf turned my dad into a liar at times too.

"What'd you shoot, Dad?"

If he said 82, that usually meant 85.

Or if you want a clue that maybe the back nine did not go so good, he would tell you he shot a 39 on the front. That meant he didn't want to talk about the back nine.

No problem. Me neither.

In court we swear witnesses to "tell the truth, the whole truth, and nothing but the truth, so help you God." When Ford said he shot a 39 on the front nine, it was the truth but not the whole truth.

Sinless perfection is only possible for people who have never known a 5-iron.

They say that golf is great because it is a game of tremendous integrity. Players call penalties on themselves. No referees. It is a game for gentlemen.

Personally, my experience is that much of that is aristocratic and arrogant nonsense. Most golfers have cheated.

Few people mark their ball correctly. Lots of people nudge it just a little. Many a man, me included, has stepped behind his ball to get the grass to lie down just a little.

It's one of those "venial sins," as my Catholic friends would say. Golf is full of sinners pretending to be righteous.

Most golfers who say they play by the rules—putt them out and play them exactly as they lie—shoot about four to ten strokes higher when forced to actually do just that.

Ford was one of those who enjoyed golf too much to let a bad break ruin it. Why shoot 84 when a nudge here and there could make it a 79?

17

*- 'I CAN'T BELIEVE I HIT
A 7-IRON THAT FAR!' -*

A REAL MAN

*...a good soldier of
Christ Jesus.*
2 Timothy 2:3

Golf was also a way for Ford to prove his manhood. He thought of himself as—and really was—a man, with all that means.

He joined the Marines in 1942 and stayed for 39 months without seeing his wife or coming home.

He was the breadwinner for the family.

He drove big cars. And he drove them too fast.

So when golf seduced him, he found a game that enabled him to prove he was a man.

He loved to hit a ball long over the green. I guess because he knew sinners "fall short," he was always happy, or so it seemed, to be over a green.

I can still hear him bragging, supposedly talking to himself, but loud enough for all to hear, "I can't believe I hit that 7-iron over the green."

In Ford's world, a bogey from over the green was better than a par from the front bunker.

Even landing in water because he hit the ball too far made

him almost happy. "I can't believe I hit it that far." He acted mad, but he was actually very proud to know he hit his 3-wood that far.

Same for hooks of all kinds.

He somehow knew that bad golfers hit weak slices, and that good golfers and real men hit it right to left and long. He loved Arnold Palmer's style.

So a hook into the left woods was the moral equivalent, if not superior, to a fade down the middle.

"I can't believe I ran out of fairway down there," he'd say, looking to his left into a creek.

Real men go left.

For Ford, women had no business on the course. He was not politically correct. Women in front of him almost always brought out a statement to his companions about women and their place in the game of golf, which for him was mostly back in the front yard mowing the grass, like Ginny. I often cringed when he was around women, just hoping he would decide to remain silent.

This game was for men. Real men who can hit it left and long.

18

'I'M COMING AFTER YOU NOW' -
THREE POINTS
A HOLE

"A man's enemies will be the members of his own household."
Matthew 10:36

T<small>HE BEST THING ABOUT</small> F<small>ORD</small> was simply that he absolutely loved golf more than anyone I ever knew. He also loved to compete.

There was always a competition with a partner. No money was needed to play for blood. So no money changed hands, but Ford was as competitive over nothing as most people would be for $100.

In Ford's game, it was one point for low ball, one for low total, and one for a birdie. Three points on each hole was possible.

No one got strokes. That never seemed fair. Man to man. Even to this day games where people "get strokes" do not seem right to me. A man with a 16 handicap should never be allowed to win a tournament, or so it seems to me. If a bad golfer wants to win, he needs to get better. That was Ford's philosophy, and I liked it then and now. He would rather lose man-to-man than win because a scorecard gave him strokes.

So if the match was lost by the fifteenth tee—and it usually was—he would turn to his partner, usually his younger brother, my Uncle Jule, and say, "OK, Jule, I'm coming after *you* now. How do we stand?"

He had to beat someone.

Or at least hit one long and left, even if it went into a swimming pool.

If he lost all the games, you might hear him snare some form of victory from the day by talking out loud in the car on the way home: "Man, I still can't believe I hit that 7-iron over the green on eighteen."

I learned to respond with a, "Yeah, you really hit that one," which made him puff up just a little and made supper taste better that night.

19

- 'SHOT ME A LITTLE 41' -

UNCLE JULE

*There were 700 select troops
who were left-handed, each
of whom could sling a stone
at a hair and not miss.*
Judges 20:16

I HAVE BRIEFLY MENTIONED Ford's main playing companion, his younger brother Jule. Ford infected him with the golf bug too.

Jule owned a Gulf gas station. He went to the eighth grade and was 12 years younger than Ford. Ford was the oldest of eight kids. Jule was number seven. He also had beaten the alcohol demons, like all Philpots. I vividly recall having to work at the gas station on a weekend when Uncle Jule had gone off "on a drunk." I also remember when he quit, by the grace of God, and never went back to the bottle. He needed one of those God mulligans and he got it.

He was a lefty, which made perfect sense for someone who had tobacco juice drooling out of one corner of his mouth during most golf swings. He was also like Ford, in that golf gave him a good reason to show off his good looking legs with some snazzy shorts.

I was present for his first golf game, which added up to at least 130 strokes. He got his money's worth.

He had the biggest slice known to man, but over many years he learned how to "manage" it, if there is such a thing. He finally was breaking 90 and loved it way too much.

I WOULD STOP BY THE STATION for some gas and conversation.

"How's Tim?" Not "How ya doing?" but "How's Tim?"

"Good, Uncle Jule. You play yesterday?" We all knew what game was being played. No mention of the word golf was needed, because it was the only game.

"Yep. Shot me a little 41 on the front," he'd giggle quietly and spit into a cup.

He and Ford had the same issue. Bad nines went unmentioned and good ones were proudly discussed.

He chewed tobacco all day every day. Golf was good for Jule because it was outdoors and cups were not required.

I can still hear him giggle like a little girl over a good putt. He and Ford are probably playing today, and if the team match is over they are playing each other to the clubhouse so that someone can win something.

Bagger Vance said that, "Golf is a game that cannot be won, only played." But Bagger never met Ford and Jule.

Someone has to win every day.

20

- 'LET'S PRAY' -
UNCLE DAN
"He will pray for you
and you will live."
Genesis 20:7

UNCLE DAN NEVER PLAYED GOLF. This is probably why he was the sanest and most normal guy in the Philpot family.

I have often said I'd rather hear him pray than anyone else preach. He knew God.

He also went to the eighth grade only. No seminary. No high school. His education came in World War II, where he faced the worst of the fighting in Italy. Like most of our war heroes, he wouldn't talk about it.

He had grease under his fingernails. He ran the Shell station (later Chevron) in Wilmore. Washing windshields and doing lube jobs. A coin laundry was attached and he always had lots of quarters.

Seminary students always got "credit" from him, so when he died in 1989 at age 66, they owed him a ton of money. The "preacher boys" took advantage of him, but he knew what was happening so I suppose it's OK.

He had no estate to settle because he had nothing except

the trailer he and Aunt Jimmie lived in. They raised their three daughters there.

They seemed poor to me in my childlike ways. Dad was the big shot preacher, while his three brothers were all gas station men with eighth grade educations.

When Dan died, Aunt Jimmie knew he had a box at the bank and hoped that maybe he had some money hidden or a CD of some kind. Maybe they weren't poor after all. I went to the bank for her and found his "treasures."

Sermon notes.

He had nothing in his security box but sermon notes.

Some from Ford.

Some from his pastor, David Seamands.

Some of his own, since he often went to small country churches on weekends to preach himself or just be there to pray for some other lay preacher who would do the preaching.

Sermon notes.

Several men have told me stories of Uncle Dan at the service station, seen praying with someone.

Got a problem? "Let's pray and see what God does."

No money today? "No problem. Fill 'er up and we will catch you later."

Why is it that often the poorest people are the most generous ones?

Perhaps there exists a "treasure" that supposedly rich people know nothing about. I believe that. For sure.

This simple man who went to heaven too young showed me how to pray and how to live.

Golf never ruined him.

21

- FORD'S DREAM COME TRUE -
SUGAR MILL

*"He will establish himself in
the beautiful land."*
Daniel 11:16

IN ABOUT 1967 A DENTIST IN FLORIDA gave Ford's ministry some land near New Smyrna, Florida. Dr. Jones must have gotten a nice tax deduction.

Ford sure did not need 400 acres of swampland in the middle of nowhere, but he did always need money for the work, so he took the land with the idea of selling it. But then came the brainstorm to build a golf course.

Ford had a dream. The ministry sold the land for some much needed money to a group of his friends who would build a first-class golf course. Ford's dream could come true. He would not own anything, but he would feel connected to the course and have input into the operation. Or so he thought.

A famous golf course architect of that time, Joe Lee, was hired.

Bill Nutting from Lookout Mountain Country Club in Chattanooga was hired as the golf professional.

Sugar Mill Golf Club became a reality. In 1969 the course

opened to rave reviews.

Alligators… jungle… over 7,000 yards long. I must have played it a hundred times and never broke par. I lost hundreds of balata balls there. It was one of the hardest courses in Florida.

In 1971, Sue and I married and off we went to Daytona Beach for our honeymoon, on July 31. By the way, yes, you might be a redneck if you go to Daytona Beach, Florida, in the first week of August for a honeymoon.

And yes, I am now embarrassed to say that I played golf at Sugar Mill on my honeymoon. But to my credit, not every day. And to my further credit, Sue went with me at least one day.

I have never cheated on my wife unless you count golf. But what kind of man-boy would cheat on his honeymoon? *Ouch!*

Sugar Mill was a huge success. The club quickly got on all the lists of best courses in Florida. It was used for PGA Tour qualifying. But it was so hard that some didn't like it. If you did not hit it straight, you just simply lost your ball. Some poor souls needed a dozen balls.

But Ford was in his glory telling people about the course he built. You would have thought he was the designer himself.

In his mind, he was. Some dreams come true.

22

- 'YOU NEED TO HANG ON' -

GOLF CARTS

*He jammed the wheels
of their chariots so they had
difficulty driving.*
Exodus 14:25

Ford was a maniac in a golf cart. It was merely a reflection of how he drove automobiles. He should have been a NASCAR driver. He amassed a fine collection of speeding tickets and was a big believer in tailgating—and I don't mean the kind in the parking lot before a football game.

"Preacher, slow down," is a phrase which I heard many times after Ford had explained to the cop who he was. They often let him go.

In golf, you were not one of his true friends unless he had thrown you out of the cart. He loved hard left turns, which meant the passenger went flying out the right side.

He usually would not even notice he was alone for a few seconds.

Then, as one might expect, he'd want to know what happened. "Where are you?" he'd say, implying that the entire thing was your fault.

"You need to hang on" was another phrase I recall—

although he knew nothing about hanging on because I never recall him being a passenger.

He always drove. He was a man in control. He drove.

He also, of course, ignored all signs, such as "Stay on Path Today."

Those signs were for other lower beings. Cart path rules did not apply to preachers.

He especially hated to have to stay 20 yards away from the greens and tees. I have seen him pull up so close that his first step out of the cart—which might be still moving—would be onto the surface of the green.

One famous incident occurred at Spring Valley Country Club when they had new fancy carts that braked automatically. Just let off the accelerator and the cart would brake by itself.

Somehow, though, the system failed. Ford and the cart somehow got mixed up and the cart went flying into a creek on the fourteenth hole, all while Ford was out and running toward the cart. Not to save it from drowning. To grab his 3-wood.

He hit his shot before even thinking about what to do about a cart in the creek upside down. The cart was expendable, but not his golf game.

Only after hitting his shot did he even wonder what happened to the cart. "I knew this was a bad idea," he said. He was right about that.

I have followed in his footsteps and I also hate cart paths. To me, blacktop on a golf course is about as ugly as it gets. And what can be worse than playing golf with "Cart Path Only" rules when the path is usually on the right and I am trying to get rid of my hook?

Like Ford, I also like to hit it long and left. Not good for "Cart Path Only" days.

23

- 'GOLF HELPS' -

BOB NELSON

*The Spirit helps us in
our weakness.*
Romans 8:26

FORD HAD DISCIPLES.

The assistant professional at Tates Creek in 1966, and therefore a protégé of Humzey Yessin as well, was Bob Nelson. He was a cocky young alcoholic who had no reason to be cocky, but was anyway. You know the type.

The story of how he became one of Ford's disciples, and eventually an evangelist himself, is fascinating for sure. He died suddenly on March 18, 2008, leaving behind his wife Ann, three daughters, and several grandchildren.

He was a PGA professional and Methodist evangelist.

Oxymoron.

Someone can research this, but my guess would be that Bob was literally the only such combination in history. Sort of like a marathon champion and a couch potato. Not likely to happen.

In 1965, Bob was the 25-year-old assistant pro at Tates Creek. He may have given me my first lesson, but it would have been in-between drinks and I do not remember it. He only remembered it after I was winning some tournaments and he took some small credit.

In 1975, Bob was a 35-year-old head golf pro at London Country Club in Kentucky. He weighed 120 pounds dripping wet and was a full-blown alcoholic. Even his drinking buddies worried about him.

But then he met Christ. The club champion at London was a Christian car dealer (another oxymoron), Howard Jones, whom Bob respected. In the club's parking lot, he prayed with Bob to trust Christ. Bob's run with booze was over. He was empty.

A month later, an evangelist who loved golf, Ford Philpot, came to town and nailed it down in an old-fashioned revival at Laurel County High School. The invitation was given and Bob publicly let the world know that he would follow Jesus.

He started college as a freshman at age 35. By 42, he was a pastor and evangelist. During those seven years he worked for Ford as an "associate evangelist," learning from the master.

MANY OF HIS OLD FRIENDS from the bars and golf shops kept waiting for Bob to fall off the wagon, but 33 years later he was still following Jesus when he died of a sudden heart attack.

Bob left extensive notes about what to do and say at his funeral. He had a button on his computer that said simply, "When I die." His wonderful wife, Ann, punched the button and a lot of memorable statements appeared.

His most profound statement for me was the simplest: "GOLF HELPS."

He knew non-golfers would not understand, but he didn't care. He knew golfers would understand.

His new and dramatic love of God in 1975 did not change his old love—golf!

He knew that "golf helps."

Why?

Golf meant being with people you like.

Golf meant being outside, smelling grass, hearing birds, feeling wind.

Golf meant confronting your own weaknesses as a player. Golf meant feeling like Arnold Palmer at the Masters when you made a long putt.

Golf meant imagining you were better than you really were once upon a time.

Bob pastored several churches, but after he retired he worked at Dick's Sporting Goods, selling clubs and being Jesus to those who came in the store.

He wept over the loss of persimmon woods, but thrilled like all of us at the newfound ability to hit longer drives with the new equipment.

He could convince you that a new driver or putter would change your life. You would never miss another putt, if you listened to Bob. Your life in the rough was over, in the gospel according to Bob. Nothing but fairways from here on out.

At heart, Bob was a salesman, selling Jesus to anyone who would listen, or a golf club to those who would not.

So, don't forget: Golf helps.

Smell the grass, feel the wind, hear the birds. Spend time with friends. And don't forget the God who made it all possible.

He learned most of that from Ford.

24

- 'YEAH, FOUR BYPASSES' -
HYPOCHONDRIAC

"Master, the one you love
is sick."
John 11:3

F ORD LOVED DOCTORS. He often stated that he wished he had been a medical missionary. I would kindly remind him that such was not possible without medical school. His mediocre GPA would not have impressed medical schools.

My mother Virginia was a summa cum laude person, literally. She had a 3.97 in college. Pretty good for someone who started college at age 33. Not Ford, who started at age 30, being three years younger than Ginny. His GPA was, like his sons' grades, mostly unmentioned.

He was especially thrilled, therefore, when Asbury College gave him an honorary doctorate. Even though he failed to graduate high school. Even though he got into college by talking his way in and finally graduated with average grades.

He was now officially Dr. Philpot. He loved that designation. His close friends even called him "Doc."

He would even pretend to be a real doctor if someone thought he was a real doctor. On occasion, a travelling companion would call him "Doc" and the next thing you know he would be giving medical advice to his fellow passengers.

I actually saw him give nitroglycerine to a woman with chest pains one time. I was a lawyer by then. I started to say something, but it was too late.

We were on an airplane. "Ma'am, just slip this under your tongue and let me know if you have any more problems," he said to a lady sitting in Aisle 23B of a Delta flight. I suppose you can't be sued for malpractice if you're not a real doctor.

HE LOVED GOING TO NEW PLACES where he could talk to strangers about his ailments.

He was fully aware that I was not interested, so he was always looking for someone else to talk health issues with. My wife, Sue, was often the recipient of Ford's latest medical report. She was a registered nurse, so she knew too much. And she has the spiritual gift of mercy, so she would listen and moan sympathetically at just the right time.

But a stranger was even better.

For instance, when we went to Scotland to play golf, he was by then 67 years old and a seasoned hypochondriac. Open heart surgery in 1977 was all the proof he needed that he really was sick.

Want to be his friend? Just ask him about that scar on his chest.

He always managed to wear golf shirts with the top three buttons undone, even in cold and rainy Scotland.

"Yeah, four bypasses," he would say.

This offered the chance to tell anyone who would listen that he played a lot better before he had the heart trouble.

Not true. But it sure sounded good. Especially in Scotland. The farther away he got from home, the better his game used to be. Me too.

25

- 'NICE BROCHURE' -
HAMPDEN DUBOSE ACADEMY

*Bring up your children
in the nurture of the Lord.*
Ephesians 6:4

In 1965, Ford and Virginia decided to send me to a boarding school for some reason. I was 14, so I was skinny, a smart aleck, and mischievous. I was not a bad kid.

But apparently Ford and Virginia were happy to see me go.

So off I went to Florida to Hampden DuBose Academy near Zellwood, Florida. It was located in an orange grove, so it was likely the nicest smelling campus in the U.S.A.

This was a school mostly for "missionary kids." Parents who were busy saving souls and fixing the world sent their kids to HDA. Billy Graham's kids even went there.

Leaving home and going to Florida for ninth grade sounded like a great idea. It was a small school with about a hundred students.

No snow. They had a nice brochure. It showed a huge lake for swimming and skiing and so forth. Warm weather all year. Tennis. Sports of all kinds all the time.

Girls, too. Although, at age 14, I knew nothing about the

female species. Ford never gave me anything close to the birds-and-bees talk. He had decided to let me figure that one out on my own. Probably like his dad did.

The brochure even showed "golf."

When I arrived in the fall of 1965, I found no golf course. Turns out it was a flag stuck in a field near an orange grove with the intent to deceive kids like me into thinking that I would be playing golf in Florida. Instead, I didn't touch a club for two years.

I found the sports fields that looked so great on the brochure were pretty rough. The lake was pretty, but we did not get in the water much. Gators lived there.

It was created more for the brochure than for the kids.

They gave every kid a job and I learned for the first time that the philosophy of the school was that every student should work. On top of the classes, I was now waiting tables. I can still carry six plates on one arm, or wash dishes, or weed a garden. All thanks to HDA.

And I was in a room with three other boys. My fellow freshman was Stevie Saint, the son of famous martyred missionary Nate Saint. We became best friends and helped each other survive by watching out for each other as we broke as many rules as possible.

Breaking rules was actually pretty easy, because they had lots of rules.

This was a "Christian" high school. I use that word loosely. It was religious, but I am not sure about the Christian part. We went to "church" 13 times a week. Every weekday morning was chapel. Every weekday night was Vespers. And three times on Sunday. We sang as a big choir for the community every Sunday afternoon. I can still sing the tenor part to the "Hallelujah" chorus in my sleep. Or, I should say, I can hear it. I can't hit the notes anymore.

But the problem is that the Christian message was being modeled by very non-Christian adults. I first heard the *n-word* from the elderly Mrs. DuBose, who announced to us that "Communist n------" had been on campus.

And then I caught the DuBose administrators opening mail from my parents. That's when I finally got up the nerve to figure out how to call home secretly and tell Ford what was really going on. He caught a plane to Florida and I didn't stay much longer. I was back in public school for my junior and senior years.

26

- 'WOULD YOU LIKE TO GO TO VESPERS?' -
DATING

She was an intelligent and beautiful woman.
1 Samuel 25:3

HAMPDEN DUBOSE ACADEMY did have one positive. Sue Davis showed up during my second year and we began to date!

Dating at HDA was bizarre.

It was like golf in that that they had lots of rules that made no sense. They had a rule that each student had to date once a week. But no touching. No kissing. No hand holding. Dates were for Sunday night Vespers and ice cream to follow.

We were given Southern-style lessons in etiquette. Dress. Politeness. How to treat a woman. Those sorts of things. I tried but was not very good at it. But it was good stuff to learn.

LOCATED ON A WALL IN THE KITCHEN was a list. On the list was the name of every girl in the school. A brand new list went up every Monday morning. The idea was to write your name next to the girl's name after you had asked her for a date.

She was not allowed to say no. She had to accept. Another crazy rule.

Monday morning at breakfast was the optimum moment to ask. That nailed it down and you did not have to worry about it all week. You could not "date" the same girl two weeks in a row, so if you had a girlfriend, you had an "off" date and an "on" date.

There were about five more girls than boys in the school, so every Sunday night was an odd sight, with the entire student body sitting as couples except for the five or so lonely hearts. These girls were an odd assortment of overweight and underweight beauties who were filled with mixed emotions.

I would presume they were sad that no one asked them for a date, but happy that they did not have to endure an evening with idiots like me.

Pain to a girl's self-esteem from lacking a date was countered by sheer joy that the fat kid with the thick glasses who slobbered and stammered had asked someone else for the romance of Vespers and ice cream.

When school started in the fall, they would give you time to get ready for the big first date night. Several weeks of anticipation and preparation went into that first week. There were no dates for about two months, as the newcomers had to get accustomed to the school and all of its ridiculous rules.

As a ninth grader, I was about 5 feet, 8 inches tall and 125 pounds. I definitely had never had a "date." I knew nothing about girls. I had no sister. Females were a total mystery. Still are, actually.

FORD AND VIRGINIA WERE OLD SCHOOL in sex education and had told me absolutely nothing. If they had sat me down to talk about the birds and the bees, I would have thought they were talking about real birds and real bees. Sex was a foreign subject. I cannot imagine a more naïve 14-year-old ninth grader than I was in 1965.

And yet I was now supposed to go on a "date." I was petrified. I was shaking like a bad putter with a left-to-right four-footer to get into heaven.

I had no understanding that Monday morning was the time to ask a cute girl if she would like to go to Vespers on Sunday night.

Instead, I waited until about Thursday to even look at the kitchen list. It was almost completely full. Perhaps eight names were blank.

Who were these prizes on the board? How would I figure out who would be my first date? I felt like an NFL general manager who has traded away all his draft choices. Now he is looking for some prize to draft in the eighth round. Slim pickings.

On one hand I could go for the pimply faced little freshman who was surely destined to become a nun. Or perhaps the bookworm whose thick glasses made her look eerily like a fly. My mind was swirling.

I decided to pray: "God, if you are really there, let there be a cute little thing that somehow slipped through the cracks down to the eighth round." I wanted a Tom Brady with lipstick and a skirt. Surely someone had fallen down the list unnoticed who would make a good first date for Timmy Philpot.

I did not even know enough to be mad at Ford and Virginia for totally failing to train me, for sending me 800 miles away from home, for abandoning me.

I went back Friday afternoon and noticed that the list was now down to six. Every single guy in the school had a date except me. I was the last hope for those six girls.

I have no memory of the name of the girl I chose. I do know that I personally inspected all six prospects at Friday night dinner. I was a waiter that night. I could walk around and pretend to be working when in fact I was checking out the prospects.

My final choice was a senior. She was four inches taller than me. I looked up at her at breakfast Saturday morning and asked, "Would you like to go to Vespers with me on Sunday night?"

She must have had mixed emotions. She would not be stuck in the back row. But she would be stuck with a pipsqueak named Philpot.

And she was not allowed to say no. So I don't know if she was happy or sad.

In hindsight, it was the perfect first date. Sort of like going with your mother to a movie.

The good news is that by the next year I was an old pro at this dating thing. That is when Sue Davis appeared on the scene. She was a real missionary kid, who had been growing up in Africa. Her father Billy and my dad Ford were best friends and must have conspired at least a little to hook up their kids.

Our first real time together was on the plane to Florida. We sat together and I got airsick and puked on the plane. She had kicked off her shoes and I grabbed the left one for an airsickness bag. She was not impressed.

But even though the first impression I made on Sue was less than stellar, I was ready to make my comeback. By the tenth grade, I had been through the wars and was now a dating machine. I knew that Monday morning breakfast was the time to find Sue and ask her for the first date.

To my horror, she had already been asked by another guy who also knew the deal. She couldn't say no.

So I had to wait until the second week to get my first real

date with Sue Davis, the girl I already knew could be my wife. And now, 41 years of our marriage later, she still looks good.

Thanks, HDA.

27

MR. ABNEY

Bless and do not curse.
Romans 12:14

AFTER BEING IN FLORIDA FOR TWO YEARS, I was happy to get home in 1967 and take up golf again.

My coach at Tates Creek High School was Bob Abney. He was an old basketball coach who shot about 95 on a good day of golf. We had one of the best teams in the state and he thought he was responsible. All the kids on the team would play college golf.

He was sure he had "coached 'em up." What he actually did was drive the van.

He talked with an odd lisp which made everything he said funny. He cussed like a sailor, but told us not to: "G-- d-----, boys, stop that cussin.'" Very convincing.

As a junior, I was fifth man on a four-man team. But then I got lucky. Mike Smith, our best player, came up ineligible. I finally made it as a senior to fourth man.

There I was, with three really good sophomores, all of whom were better than me and destined for college golf. We won the regional and headed for state competition.

We would have state won, too, except a couple of our hotshots ballooned into the 80s the final day. And my own 80 didn't help anything either.

We blew a lead and came in third, but Mr. Abney's tirade was almost worth losing to hear. He thought it was still basketball and golfers would react like his basketball players did to a great halftime speech.

He forgot it was not halftime. It was over.

He also forgot that we didn't care.

Or at least we acted that way.

28

- 'SON, I'M PROUD OF YOU' -

DANNY

*"You are my Son; today I
have become your Father."*
Hebrews 5:5

My brother Danny was a real athlete and therefore played football and baseball instead of golf. If you want to be a good golfer, being a good athlete can actually be a curse, since you become a star at the real sports.

Being a football star is logical at age 16, but not as profitable at age 40 when football injuries are kicking in.

Age 40 is perfect for golf, but really old for football.

Ford was a fallen human in many ways. Like most men, that shows up the most in how to be a father.

Danny now relates that Ford only one time told him he was "proud" of him. Danny was captain of the football team his senior year. Ford was busy saving the world and therefore never went to a game until Danny's last game as a senior. Going to every game seems pretty unimportant when you think the fate of souls is at stake.

Danny walked out for the coin flip in the big game. Both teams were 9-0 and now playing for the district championship. After the game, which Danny's team lost, Dad said, "I was sure proud of you when I saw you walking out for the coin flip to start the game."

And Danny wondered: *Fine, but where you been for the last three years, anyway?*

He had not been to a single game in three years. This is quite a painful lesson in fatherhood.

Ford was a wonderful man and father.

But Danny still is moved to the verge of tears when he recounts how his father was not there for his games—yes, even 40 years later.

And it really did not matter that he was gone doing a good thing, preaching.

Missing the games from drinking too much or preaching too much is still missing the game.

Kids don't really care *why*. They do care *where*, as in, "Where were you, Dad?"

So Ford wasn't perfect. But now, more than 40 years later, Danny and I have decided that he was the perfect father for us. And that's good enough.

Part of the good news of Ford missing Danny's games was that Danny's own son Parker never played a baseball or football game without his dad in the stands or on the sidelines or in the dugout. When Parker walked on the Alabama football team and ended up with a national championship ring, Danny was the proudest father in the New Orleans Superdome, even though Parker was on the sidelines. The uniform said "16 Philpot," and Danny was a proud papa.

It would not have happened without a good dad who remembered the bad feelings of a missing dad, and the good feelings of a dad in the stands. It would not have happened if Danny had been too busy. He was not perfect, but he was there. That counts for something.

One of Ford's flaws was that no matter how much he

loved being a dad, he still thought being a preacher was more important.

In Ford's theology, family sacrifices were required. Lost souls in places like Ft. Wayne, Indiana, were more important than Friday night football games.

I'm not sure.

As God's plan turned out, Sue and I have no kids, so I'm no expert.

But Ford may have been wrong about that.

29

- HOWARD, JOHNNY, MARVIN, WALLY, BUDDY, AND MAC -
OTHER HEROES

They were the heroes of old, men of renown.
Genesis 6:4

THE BEST PLAYER BY FAR of all Ford's buddies was Howard Jones, the man who prayed with Bob Nelson in the parking lot of the London Country Club. He was just plain good. He hit the golf ball so solid. But no one knew it because he would not play golf on Sundays, and therefore most tournaments were not possible for him.

When I was a college golfer and thought I was pretty good, Howard was over 60 and would beat me every time. Every time.

A five-minute lesson from him after my senior year of college got me hitting the ball the best of my life. He showed me how to hit a draw. My gentle fade had turned into a slice and he fixed it in five minutes.

BEYOND HOWARD, it was the best players in my hometown of Lexington who were heroes of sorts.

In hindsight, I realize that these guys were not all that good, compared to Nicklaus and Palmer and Casper and Player. But their names were in the paper for local golf tournaments and, without knowing it, I aspired to be like them. Palmer was out of reach, but not these guys.

I liked the idea of seeing my name in the paper. My first recollection of that was an interclub match in 1967. I was a skinny 16-year-old, playing in the "B" division. I shot 87.

But I got my picture in the paper, along with six other kids. I liked that.

Ego is an awful curse.

I played in my first city tournament a year or two later and recall seeing Wally Rose and Alton "Mac" McPherson coming up the ninth fairway at Lexington Country Club.

I thought, *Wow, there they are. I've read their names in the paper so they must be good.*

Johnny Owens was without a doubt the gold standard of amateur golf in Kentucky. He not only won the state amateur tournament in the 1950s but also played in a U.S. Open, played in the Masters one year, nearly won the U.S. Amateur a couple of times, and of course won the Lexington City tournament ten times.

Marvin Lear was harder for a kid to like because he was a stickler for the rules. He would lie on the ground to read a putt. He hit it short but straight. And he called penalties on opponents. But he could play and I learned to love him.

Wally Rose was a local mailman and such a competitor that he literally was almost murdered on the eighteenth green at Spring Valley by a betting companion whom he accused of cheating. The guy dragged him into a bunker and tried to kill him with a putter to the head. The guy went to jail.

It was always a mistake to ask Wally how he was doing, at least during the golf season.

"Hi, Wally, how's it going?" You knew as soon as you said it you had made a mistake.

"Well, I am putting really good right now, but I am not hitting my driver very good. Even though I hit a good drive on number one, and hit an 8-iron to 12 feet, I lipped out the putt. On two, I drove it into the rough and missed the green but got it up and down. On three..." On and on.

Buddy Mahan was a true gentleman golfer. He was good enough that when Arnold Palmer came for an exhibition in the 1960s to Winchester Country Club, the only logical choice to play with Arnie was Buddy Mahan, who had been club champion a million times.

Buddy also saved Wally's life when he pulled the putter-wielding assailant off him in that bunker at Spring Valley.

"Mac" was simply the greatest putter I have ever seen.

About 5 feet, 6 inches tall, he hit his driver about 220 max. He would often beat me when he was hitting a 4-wood to the green while I hit a 9-iron or wedge.

We travelled to Venezuela and Scotland together and he became one of my main spiritual "projects." He never went to church from the time he was 10 years old until he came to hear me "preach" one time.

His wife was a wonderful churchgoing woman. I made a deal with her: "You pray for Mac and I will play with him. Somehow, we will get him to heaven." I'm still hoping it works.

We exchanged lessons with each other. I would give him some spiritual tips on occasion (like simple trust in Jesus to get to heaven) and he would help me with my golf game, especially the short game.

His tips were simple with the putter:

1. Loosen your grip
2. Open your stance slightly
3. Keep your head still and never look up.

He listened for the sound of the ball going in the cup. He never saw it. He should have been a teaching pro, but instead he sold dental equipment and played when he could. He now shoots his age every day, even though he is sick and tired most days. Golf has kept him alive.

LATER WHEN I WON THE CITY TOURNAMENT TWICE, I realized that I was "Wally" or "Johnny" or "Buddy" or "Marvin" or "Mac" to some of the younger kids. It was always nice to know that someone had read my name in the paper and therefore thought I was good.

Getting old is not so bad.

Really.

Especially when you get a chance to be a hero to someone younger.

30

- *'I'M SORRY, LITTLE FELLA'* -

ANDY BEAN

*Goliath stood and shouted,
"Choose a man and have
him come down to me."*
1 Samuel 17:8

I KEPT GETTING BETTER UNTIL FINALLY, at age 20 in 1971 and already finished with two years of college, I was offered a chance to play real college golf.

Asbury College was my home for two years and they had no golf team. We started a golf team while I was there. I shot a 69 in a match and must have done something else to get the attention of Danny McQueen, who was the Kentucky coach. He offered me a full scholarship for some reason I still don't understand. His team must have been bad.

In fact, UK was mediocre before I got there and just as mediocre after I arrived.

My career at the University of Kentucky had no highlights.

I did play with people who would later become famous. Jerry Pate comes to mind. He was playing second man for Alabama, so I presumed he couldn't be too good. I always presumed anyone playing with me couldn't be that good. After all, they were playing with *me*.

I remember him throwing a flag into the woods at the 1973 SEC Tournament at Callaway Gardens, Georgia. I forget why. I also was surprised that he won the U.S. Amateur the next year, and the U.S. Open two years after that. I guess I was wrong about how good he was.

Maybe the golf coach at Alabama was off too.

But I did actually beat Andy Bean one day. It was the opening round of the SEC Tournament in Dothan, Alabama in 1974, my last college golf tournament. I had shot a million the day before in a practice round and I was nervous. Nervous is never good in golf.

My experience is that two things make you nervous in golf.

One is when you are playing really good. You know that if you don't finish well, it is a super real "choke."

The other, and more realistic, is when you are playing bad and you know it.

You feel the train wreck coming. You are nervous because you are aware of the almost certain probability of a disaster.

That was me on the first tee in Dothan. I was so desperate that I played with a glove for the first time in my life. I had to try something different. And I used an all-wooden putter from the 1930s borrowed from one of those old heroes, Marvin Lear. The putter did not have a straight face. It was likely illegal. No one cared or noticed.

Andy Bean squeezed by hand on the first tee and for a moment I thought he had broken a bone. He seemed huge.

He was an All-American. I was me.

And then it happened. I birdied the first three holes with sizable putts. I then made a 20-foot putt for par on the fourth hole.

My adrenaline was off the charts.

I remember hitting my drive 20 yards past Andy Bean's

ball on the fifth hole. I had laid up in practice every day to avoid a pond, but now I could reach the par-5 with my trusty 5-wood. I hit a perfect shot.

I had a five-foot eagle putt to go five under par. Wow!

Do you see that? I hit a 5-wood to five feet to go five under on the par-5 fifth hole.

Really? True story.

Meanwhile, Andy Bean had a double bogey on the second hole and was three over.

ON THAT FIFTH GREEN, it was like being in the "Twilight Zone" with Rod Serling. Unfortunately, I woke up and remembered who I was. I three-putted from five feet, and then went on to survive the day with a score around par. But I beat Andy Bean, who apologized coming up the eighteenth fairway for his ranting and raving and cussing that day. He couldn't believe a nobody like me was beating him.

I remember that I overheard him tell his coach that "the little fella" was beating him. He was implying that if I hit it past him, which I did a few times, he must be playing one of the worst rounds of his life, which he was. I got back to normal the next two days with a 79 and an 80 or something like that. The old wooden putter got even older real quick.

At the end of the tournament and the end of my college career, he was still Andy Bean and I was still me.

He qualified at Q-School for the PGA Tour. I was the 77th alternate to get into law school.

College golf was great because it showed me who I was. There was no reason to try to be a pro. There was no reason to waste someone's money and my time playing the mini-tours while I got a little better.

Gary Koch's 67 was always going to be better than my 77.

Curtis Strange's 66 was way better than my 76.

Bill Kratzert's 70 was lower than my 80.

Andy North's 69 beat my 79.

This was real golf where all strokes count. I learned that law school would be much better than Q-School.

In hindsight, it's a good thing I was not a little better. I might have wasted a lot of time and money missing four-foot putts and trying to chip in for par.

I would never win a million-dollar golf tournament. But who knows? I might win a million-dollar lawsuit.

Law school beats Q-School for most.

31

- *'DAD, YOU CAN'T PICK UP'* -

CHOKING

"My only aim is to finish the race."

Acts 20:24

MEMORIES OF CHOKING HAUNT ME.
I still hate left lip four-footers because I remember missing one in a playoff at Frankfort Country Club in the Daniel Boone Invitational. And only I know for sure that I missed the putt because I choked.

Others watching may have thought, "Everyone misses four-foot putts." But I know the truth. I remember the feeling and it is not good. I choked.

I have had the very same experience hundreds of times since then.

As popularly considered, choking is what happens on the last hole or maybe the last round.

The truth, though, is that real super choking is when the choke starts on the first hole or first day and just continues for the entire event. It is usually explained as having a bad day or a bad week, when in fact it is a super choke that does not even wait until the last hole. It starts early and never goes away.

As recently as 2010, I shot 97 in a USGA Senior tournament

at Victoria National in Indiana. Of course, with my 5.1 index and the course rating, it was a net 89, so not so bad. But it would be fair to say that the course was difficult and I choked from the first tee all the way to the clubhouse.

FORD AND I EXPERIENCED THIS FIRSTHAND at the Kentucky Father-Son Tournament in about 1970 at Danville Country Club.

This seemed like a wonderful idea for two days of father-son bonding time on the golf course.

But what if the father misses a two-foot putt, leaves it on the lip, then reaches over and picks up his ball without putting out in a medal play tournament? On the first hole. So nervous he could barely breathe. He could preach in front of a 100,000 people without wavering, but a little white ball was another matter.

I remember not being as nice as I wanted to be: "Dad, you can't pick up."

He looked at me in horror. He knew I was right, but that did not mean he wanted to hear me say anything.

One of the problems with golf is that, on occasion, your worst nightmares come true. It rarely happens in real life, but in golf it seems to be pretty regular.

But we did make a discovery that day. Ford was not made for tournament golf where you post a score and putt everything out.

In fact, not many people are made for such a nerve-racking experience.

He was made for "three points a hole," beating Uncle Jule and, best of all, telling someone he just met to come hear him preach that night at the local revival.

He was a tournament preacher, not a tournament golfer.

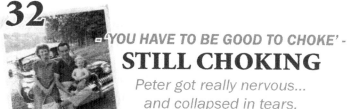

32

-'YOU HAVE TO BE GOOD TO CHOKE' -
STILL CHOKING

Peter got really nervous...
and collapsed in tears.
Mark 14:71-72 (The Message)

Y OU HAVE TO HAVE A CERTAIN AMOUNT of game to put
yourself in a position to "choke," according to the classic
definition of losing at the end.

Most players are not good enough to choke. They choke, if
you want to call it that, before the game even starts. Like Ford
and me sometimes.

For instance, I have never choked on the 72nd hole of a U.S.
Open.

Why? I was never good enough to even make it to the final
qualifier for a U.S. Open. You get the point.

Guys with double digit handicaps should not be allowed
to sit in a bar and call Greg Norman a choker. They should be
arrested. It should be a crime.

But even so, the game is great because it must be finished.
Being great for 54 or even 71 holes is not enough. You must
"finish the course."

Greg Norman at the Masters. More than once. Rory
McIlroy in 2011 at Augusta. Remember Ed Sneed?

Jean van de Velde at Carnoustie. His brain went dead even more than his muscles locked up. In fact, we almost forget he somehow made a seven-foot putt for the triple-bogey seven that got him into the playoff.

We forget that Arnold Palmer lost the Masters with a double bogey on the last hole when a par would have won.

Gary Player did the same one year.

Sam Snead made an eight on the last hole of a U.S. Open to later lose in a playoff. Kyle Stanley made the same number to lose in 2012 at San Diego.

Phil Mickelson doubled the eighteenth hole at Winged Foot. So did Colin Montgomerie the very same afternoon.

Johnny Miller won the Pebble Beach event when he was in his 40s by holding his arms instead of the club so he would not choke. Instead of holding the club with both hands, somehow he held on to the club with his left arm and then grabbed his left arm with his right hand. He looked like he was dancing with himself. Don't laugh until you have tried it. I have. It works.

And we have not even begun to discuss the tens of thousands of stories of chokes in the third flight of the local country club tournament. I once won a club tournament when my opponent missed an *eight-inch* putt, and I promise he was trying. I could tell he was choking. It was physical.

I personally have left a 12-inch putt short just from nerves. I have double hit putts due to nerves. I now often putt with my eyes closed because I am fully capable of choking at any time, on any hole, in any tournament, or even no tournament. I have choked when playing by myself on a Sunday evening. True.

Remarkably, there are no Tiger choke stories. Yet.

There is not a single Nicklaus choke story.

THE MOST HEART-WRENCHING STORY is my old friend Harcourt Kemp. He qualified for 20 USGA events, including two U.S. Opens, six U.S. Amateurs, three U.S. Mid-Amateurs, one U.S. Senior Open, one U.S. Junior, and seven U.S. Senior Amateurs. Not to mention, I know he played in the British Amateur when I was there. Plus 26 club championships at Louisville Country Club and two club championships at Valhalla Golf Club.

A legend in amateur golf. And a wonderful gentleman. A role model for guys like me who were a little younger.

Harcourt was still playing national level senior amateur golf in 2000 when he came to the last hole of a prominent event in Florida.

He came to the last hole of the 54-hole event with a six-stroke lead.

He lost.

The details are too gruesome to recite. A national golf magazine described how he "choked" in a special article on the subject.

Harcourt, if you read this, I am serious. You may have choked. But you were a good player and only good players choke.

33

- 'YOU'LL NEVER MAKE IT WITH THAT SWING' -

SQUARE TO SQUARE

There will be false teachers among you.
2 Peter 2:1

JUST LIKE FORD, I HAVE BEEN IN A LIFELONG SEARCH for improvement in golf.

In my 40s and not playing enough to have any timing, I actually bought the tapes and went to Moe Norman's Natural Golf seminar. I still think it is a great way to play if you start golf late in life and can't break 100. But at some point I realized that no one, and I mean no one, on tour plays that way. It can't be right. You use a baseball grip. You stand with a wide stance. You lift your hands higher than normal. Then, swing hard. It goes straight at first. But then the lack of talent takes over.

"Stack and Tilt" got my attention more recently. I have the CDs if you'd like to borrow them.

When I was about 23, the pro at Sugar Mill in Florida, Bill Nutting, looked me over one day. I had really never had a golf lesson. He saw I was pretty good and knew I played in college. He recognized I was still dreaming of a tour life, but also he knew it was a ridiculous dream.

He was teaching the latest and greatest method, called Square to Square.

There were one or two successful pros doing it. Their names are forgotten, which should tell you everything you need to know about Square to Square. Jim Flick was teaching it at one time. Look for late 1960s *Golf Digest* issues and you will see some articles about this bizarre method that makes sense at first glance. Here's the key tenet: Don't swing in a "circle," but keep the club head "square" throughout.

Bill showed me how to do it and I must have been a quick study because within a matter of minutes, I was a tour-quality ball striker. I was hitting 3-irons at the flag on the range. As long as Bill was there to monitor my swing, I was Jack Nicklaus.

Unfortunately, I returned to Kentucky and got stuck half way between Square to Square and my other homemade swing taught by no one.

I WAS LEFT WITH Square to Not-Square.

I couldn't hit a wedge straight. I wasn't sure until my backswing if I was going to swing Square or old-fashioned.

It actually was a blessing, because my game got so bad that turning pro became an obvious delusion.

Thanks, Bill Nutting. You may have saved my life.

34

- 'NO GIMMES' -

THE YIPS

The King was shaken...
2 Samuel 18:33

PEOPLE WHO HAVE NEVER HAD THE YIPS do not understand. I had a serious case of the yips 30 years ago and have been on the edge of them most days of my life.

For anyone not familiar, the "yips" is an almost medical condition of being unable to do a simple task, such as make a 12-inch putt.

The body freezes. The golfer may shake or experience a form of paralysis. The muscles get tight. Breathing is optional.

When I had a serious case of the yips, no one wanted to get near me. Fellow competitors don't watch. They walk away and pretend to not see what's happening. They ask you what you made on the hole because the smart ones are not watching. They have putted out and gone to the next tee so they do not have to watch the train wreck.

No one says" "pick it up." Nothing is "good."

But there is a real benefit. The best ball striking of my life by far was the year I had the yips. To shoot scores that would not embarrass me totally, I became a really good tee-to-green player. My scores did not change a lot, because I hit the ball better with everything but my putter.

Yips are not so deadly when the missed three-footer is for birdie.

The only cure I know for the yips is to start hitting it so bad that you *have* to start putting better. I accomplished that eventually. Plus I tried an orange golf ball, which was popular in the early 1980s. For some reason known only to psychologists, the orange ball cured me. It looked bigger. It did not scare me. It went in the hole a lot quicker.

I was not a hippie. I was not a yuppie. I was, however, once a yippie.

35

- 'I CAN'T GET A BACKSWING' -
NIGHTMARES

*"I had a dream that scared
me—a nightmare that
shook me."*
Daniel 4:4 (The Message)

I HAVE HAD SOME RECURRING NIGHTMARES in my life.
One involves being an adult man trying to graduate
from college. No one in the dream knows that I have not been
to class and now it is time for final exams. I have not bought
the books. I have not studied. I know nothing. I'm not even
officially enrolled. I cannot find the classroom for the final
exam.

It is usually a French exam, probably because I was
traumatized by a real D in French as a college sophomore.
I asked Mrs. Delgado how I could make a D when I made
all C's on the tests. She showed me that my grade for class
participation was an F every day. What? Every day? Apparently
I was a 25-handicap French speaker.

At some point, I wake up in a sweat extremely happy that
it was only a dream. I am not a total failure after all. I did
graduate from college and law school.

But the college exam nightmares are nothing. Golf
nightmares are the worst! Why? Because they are so

reminiscent of those nightmares that actually happen when we are wide awake on real golf courses.

GOLF NIGHTMARES FOR ME take three basic forms.

First, I am in a tournament with lots of people watching.

The space to play is cramped. I can't make a backswing because I keep hitting something. I re-tee the ball over and over and over and over. I can't find a place to tee the ball where I can get a free swing. Sometimes we are even indoors, in a hallway. The crowd watching is exasperated and starts making comments.

"Come on. Hit the ball." I turn red and explain that I can't find a good spot. I re-tee the ball until I finally wake up and realize that I am a basket case.

THE SECOND VERSION is always totally indoors.

The kitchen is the venue. Refrigerator National Golf Club. The hole is on a small table. The ball is on the vinyl floor. I have my lob wedge wide open, hitting beautiful flop shots which amaze the crowd. The ball usually lands on the table and then falls away again. I have trouble getting a backswing, too, combining the horrors of Backswing Nightmare with the Kitchen Nightmare. I usually am lying 12 by the time I wake up.

Waking up is wonderful when you lie 12.

IN MY THIRD DREAM, Late Nightmare, I am in a tournament and simply cannot make my tee time.

The venues are different, but the scene is always similar. My tee time is coming up and I am stuck in traffic. Or I am at the course but unable to get to the first tee. Or I am there but have no clubs. Or I have clubs, but I am not dressed properly so I am not fit to play. I have no shoes. Or I am in my underwear.

I need therapy.

36

- 'I DO NOT KNOW THIS MAN' -

LOU GRAHAM

"I never knew the man..."
Mark 14:71

MY MOST EMBARRASSING MOMENt with Ford was in the Atlanta airport. Of course it involved golf.

It was about 1980. Lou Graham had won the U.S. Open in 1975 and was now a fairly obscure golf pro known only to golf nuts like me. He wore a hat—I think it was an Amana refrigerator hat—on the golf course and you would have to be a real golf fan to know him.

I saw Lou standing in line to get a boarding pass. No fancy jet for Lou. Probably not even first class. No one else seemed to even know who the tall, thin, balding man was except me.

In hindsight, I should have known better, but I said: "Dad, look over there. That's Lou Graham."

"Who?"

"Lou Graham."

"Who's he?"

"He won the U.S. Open at Medinah a few years ago. You remember him, don't you?"

"Oh, sure. Lou Graham."

And of course Ford proceeded over toward Lou to introduce himself. After all, Lou would surely want to meet Ford.

If you were scripting a novel, you would now layer in the conflict. So here it is: As Ford and I were dialoging, a short stout man moved into line right behind Lou. Ford marched right up to the short man, tapped him on the shoulder and said, "Hi, aren't you Lou Graham?" to which the real Lou Graham, standing three feet away, turned and gave an odd look to the loud preacher voice behind him, while the short guy said, "No, why do you ask?"

Not embarrassed at all, Ford shouted to me across the Atlanta airport, "This isn't Lou Graham," while I attempted to die on the spot. I discovered that day that you cannot make yourself die. You need a gun or pills to do that. I wanted to say, "I do not know the man."

I pointed at the real Lou Graham.

Ford turned and chatted with him like he knew him his whole life and added, "I will never forget that U.S. Open you won."

He called me over to meet Lou Graham, introducing me as if I would not know who he was. "Lou won the U.S. Open," Ford told me.

"Oh, really?" I responded.

No embarrassment. None at all.

Oh, to be more like Ford.

Although at that moment, Ford was exactly what I never wanted to be.

37

- 'HE REALLY NEEDS THIS' -

MY GALLERY

*"'But I have
been watching...'"*
Jeremiah 7:11

FORD LIKED TO GET A GOLF CART and follow me while I played in tournaments. He was often a gallery of one. Sometimes my wife, Sue, would be his passenger.

He broke all rules about staying on the path and staying away from greens. His voice also carried way too much.

You could hear him: "He really needs this." I hated that.

Hearing him whisper was like hearing Jim Nance on a bad day in the booth.

He would, on occasion, throw Sue out of the cart by making one of his famous hard left turns. He would play "defense" by gunning his noisy gas cart before everyone had putted out. Once his son had putted out, no reason to stick around.

He would also talk bad about whoever was the opponent. Loud enough to hear.

I hated it when he said stuff like that, but I didn't know what to do about it. He was my dad.

In fact, I always had trouble being myself in his presence.

He was dad. I was son. No doubt who was in charge.

Talking back was not an option, but I could get away with silence or shutting down, which is how I handled it.

Silence was imperfect but often the only option.

Despite the emotional issues, I realized then and even now that his presence on the golf cart following showed me he cared and he loved me.

He never told me that.

I do not recall him being there when I won the Lexington City Championship. He was out preaching somewhere.

Mom, on the other hand, never followed me. She didn't need to be there and I was glad. I do recall, however, that she was standing near the eighteenth green at Spring Lake Country Club when I won the City in 1975. It was actually weird to see her standing there. Made me nervous.

Good thing I had a four-shot lead.

38

SUNDAY GOLF

*Some said, "This man is not
from God, for he does
not keep the Sabbath."*
John 9:16

THE YEAR WAS 1978. After three rounds, I was tied for the lead in the Lexington City Championship. The final round was set for Sunday, July 8. I had been playing in the tournament for many years. The leaders always teed off last, around 1 or 2 PM, sort of like the PGA Tour does.

For some mysterious reason the tee times on Sunday were set for 10:30 AM.

The officials had assured me before I even signed up that the tee times would be in the afternoon for the leaders. It mattered because I promised Danny, my preacher brother, that I would teach Sunday school on the second Sunday of his starting a new Methodist church in town.

When I discovered the conflict, I called Ford. He was home that weekend and was planning to be part of my gallery that day.

Naturally, as a lover of golf and God and not sure in which order, he offered to teach Sunday school for me and told me to go play golf.

He'd catch me on the back nine.

I thought I was off the hook. Ford had given me an OK to skip church.

But then I called my brother, the pastor. Danny paused.

He reminded me that I had promised him that I would teach. He was taking this very seriously. *Wow.*

My little brother was calling me out. I was conflicted beyond imagination.

I decided to teach and pray for rain.

Sunday morning was sunny and mild. So I pulled out of the tournament.

The newspaper headline said:

'Newton Wins with Miller on Green, Philpot in Church'

Ouch! Some religious nut on the sports page. And it was me.

Actually, it turned out better than I thought. My good friend John Newton had his biggest thrill in golf, and more than 30 years later I realize how happy I am that he won.

My new young friend Danny Miller lost in that playoff that should have never happened, but it sort of bonded him and me in a good way.

The newspaper ran a positive editorial for the first and only time about "the young Philpot" who proved "his religion meant more than golf." Not true, really, but I knew about *Chariots of Fire* and had read other scenes from the lives of the saints, so not playing a game on Sunday seemed right.

In hindsight, I think my brother and I both got caught up in the religious part of following the Sabbath God.

I am still not totally sure if I did the right thing. But I do know that at that moment I was sure I was doing the right thing, and nothing has happened in the last 33 years to change my mind.

I won the City Championship again in 1983 by making an 80-foot birdie putt on the seventeenth, and another even crazier birdie on the eighteenth to win by one. So I think the Lord and I are even on that one.

39

- ARE YOU SERIOUS? HERE? -
SCOTLAND

*"It is the rainy season;
so we cannot stand outside."*
Ezra 10:13

MY LIFELONG OBSESSION and love of links golf began at Turnberry, Scotland, in 1983.

I was not good enough to play in the British Amateur, a tournament once won by Bobby Jones, whose winner goes to the Masters.

It was mythical to even think about being there.

But somehow I was eligible in 1983 to compete in the British Amateur. And when I found out it was at Turnberry, I knew I should try to get there. I would probably embarrass myself, but I needed to go.

I was 32 years old. My prime. As good as I would ever get.

I was just a young lawyer who got to play summer golf and win a few very small tournaments on occasion. I was not good enough to win the state amateur even.

But the rules of the British Amateur said I was eligible, so off I went.

Sue and I got off the plane in Prestwick, home of the first

few British Opens. We had no hotel reservations. It was 10 days before the tournament. We were there early simply because I had no clue what to expect. This would be an adventure. And Sue was happy to come along.

We went straight to Turnberry. I walked into the pro shop and discovered the pro was Bob Erickson, whose son was married to a girl from Ashland, Kentucky!

He told me I could play for a couple of days, no problem, and no greens fees, before we headed off to see Scotland. I asked him where we could stay and instead of pointing us to a bed and breakfast somewhere, he pointed upstairs to the Dormie House, over the pro shop, with a few small rooms. He said we could stay there. Ten pounds a night.

Are you serious? Here? Right here? Go get our luggage now? At Turnberry?

The room was so pitiful it was perfect. Two twin beds. Maybe a golf picture on the wall. A smallish bathroom with old fixtures. A shower that dripped cold water which eventually got warm, but not American-style hot.

You could almost smell Bobby Locke. Or even Harry Vardon. Jack Nicklaus' 1977 loss to Tom Watson was only six years earlier, so the aroma of those two titans was lingering in the air. The "Duel in the Sun" was whispered about with awe. Nicklaus shot 65-66 on the weekend and still lost to a young Watson.

Those stars would have stayed in the gigantic white hotel on top of the hill, but the Dormie House was for real golfers, not legendary figures who, in some odd ways, don't even really exist except in our imaginations.

Sue and I pulled the twin beds together so we could snuggle all night. This is not just because we were still in love, but also because the Scots know very little about heat. It was late May, but the calendar means nothing in Scotland. The Scots have no regard for seasons and calendars.

So the next morning, at about 5:30, I was standing on the first tee at Turnberry in 45-degree weather, by myself, in a jetlagged stupor, hitting a drive down the fairway and commencing the most pure round of golf I have ever played.

By myself.

All alone.

Early morning on a world-class golf course.

Carrying my own clubs.

Pure golf.

I imagined Nicklaus and Watson. Watson won, but Nicklaus was truly great. Third place cowered 10 strokes behind them.

SOMEHOW, THE PUREST MOMENT THAT MORNING was near the twelfth tee. The Ailsa course at Turnberry winds out and along the ocean with spectacular holes beginning on four and ending on eleven. All holes from the fourth to the eleventh have the ocean on the left. Walking by myself that morning was like my first day in heaven.

Behind the eleventh green and twelfth tee was nothing but a coastal farm with an unkempt fence.

On the other side of the fence stood a singular cow.

Munching away at about 7:30 AM. Cold. Misty. No sounds except the ocean below the cliffs. The wind blowing.

As a human being, I was all alone. But the cow offered to be my new friend. He interrupted his morning breakfast of grass to stare at me. We talked.

The cow seemed to be asking, "What are you doing here? Isn't it a little early for golfers? What's with the silly hat with a woolen ball on top? Well, nice to meet you. Good luck. Cheerio."

I realized that this cow had it made. If you have to be a

cow, the field behind the twelfth tee at Turnberry is heaven. Sure beats a butcher shop in Kansas City. At that moment the cow was as magnificent as the Atlantic Ocean.

By the time I made it back to the pro shop, I knew I was in love. Links golf would be my mistress.

40

- PHILIP PARKIN -

DREAMS OF AUGUSTA

*...for their delusions
come to nothing.
Psalm 119:118*

A ND THEN, TO MAKE IT A TRUE LOVE AFFAIR, I played the best golf of my life in the real tournament.

I shot 75 on the first day of qualifying on a windy, cold, blustery day when literally no one shot par and almost everyone was in the 80s. I easily qualified through the 36 holes of qualifying for match play after a 73 the next day on the easier Arran course. I realize that 148 doesn't sound so great, but remember that this was Tim Philpot, not Tom Watson.

My brother-in-law Steve Davis had travelled all the way from Florida to be my caddie. He was in total shock because he knew I wasn't that good.

In the first round, I played Ed McGoldrick and beat him 5-and-4.

Maybe you've never heard of Ed. That is because no one has ever heard of Ed. He was more nervous than I was. He was about my age, from Long Island, New York. He and I were just glad to be there.

I sent him home. *Wow!*

I was now in the final 32 of the British Amateur.

Five more wins and I could play in the Masters! I just needed five men to have a really bad day and I was there. In match play, anyone can win, even me.

IN THE SECOND ROUND, I got to play the favorite of the British bookies, 20-year-old Philip Parkin, described in golf magazines at the time as "a sure bet to be a superstar." He was the Rory McIlroy of his day—a "pro" playing with amateurs.

In hindsight, I realize that that match was the only time in my personal history that bookies in England—and who knows, maybe Las Vegas—were taking bets on Philpot. The odds must have been stupendous. Parkin was a lock cinch. I must have been a 500-to-1 shot. I'd love to know what it really was.

But I was happy to get to play Parkin. Two weeks in the cold and rain of Scotland had turned me into a ball striking machine and a delusional idiot.

Philip had been medalist in qualifying. He was from Wales and the star of the Walker Cup, played the week before. An All-American at Texas A&M, he was turning pro after the tournament.

I was returning to Kentucky to try to win my club championship.

He was headed to the PGA Tour, hoping to make millions.

I was headed to the Fayette District Court, hoping my next DUI client would pay me the $500 he owed me so I could afford to make my house payment.

But on that day I was on a mission to delay Philip's march to stardom. I actually believed that I was headed to the Masters.

I was not in Philip's way. He was in my way.

My delusions got stronger when I birdied the first hole to go one up. Nine-iron to six feet. Putt dropped right in the heart.

When Philip missed the second green, I could see two up. He made a 10-foot putt to stop that.

By the fifth tee, though, I was still 1-up and feeling confident. He was lucky to only be 1-down.

I crushed a drive down the middle and hit a 3-wood on the green of the par-5. Philip did the same from twenty yards closer with some sort of iron. When I three-putted, the dream was gone.

It was about 48 degrees, raining sideways. My umbrella was in shambles. So was my golf game. All pars were precious. And I had run out of pars on the sixth tee.

By the time we reached the thirteenth green, it was over: 6-and-5, Parkin.

No nights for me in the famous Crow's Nest at Augusta National Golf Club, where all amateurs stay during the Masters week. No wandering around the haunted clubhouse at night, looking at pictures of Gene Sarazen and Bobby Jones from the 1930s. No running into Byron Nelson in the clubhouse, accidentally on purpose. No practice rounds with Jack Nicklaus or even Gay Brewer from my hometown. No green jackets. Back to my law practice and blue suits.

SOMEONE ELSE SAID IT FIRST: every shot in golf makes someone happy.

In this case, my wife was the happy one when I lost. When I returned to the clubhouse, drenched by the Scottish rain, I explained what happened. I expected her to commiserate with me and hug me. Instead, the biggest smile you have ever seen popped up. "You mean we can leave now? Yippee!"

She had had enough of cold and rain and Scotland. The

romance was gone. Turnberry and the Dormie House were not "cute" anymore. Hot tea was no longer wonderful. Scones were super at first. But the full Scottish breakfast was getting old. Walking in the rain on a golf course under an umbrella was not fun anymore.

She had not even slightly considered following me that day. She and our sister-in-law Peggy had sent my caddie Steve and me out with a "good luck" that we now knew was a fraud.

They were sitting in the clubhouse staying warm and hoping I would lose.

Sunshine was what she wanted. Our planned vacation in France had been delayed by my good play. She had fully expected, as I did too, to be gone two days ago.

When she found out I had qualified for match play, she was happy enough. But then I won my first match and she discovered we "might" be in Scotland the whole time. She began to understand that match play was a different animal. We might not make it to France at all. She was not happy.

"What? You mean you might be here all week?" she asked. Of course, her totally delusional husband confirmed that yes, indeed, we may be here all week. "I'm hitting it really good." Even caddie Steve confirmed, "He's playing awfully good."

As IT TURNED OUT, Parkin not only beat me but won the tournament and took "my spot" in the Masters the next spring. For me, it was back to court. Back to Lexington Country Club.

Parkin got in his practice round with Jack Nicklaus at Augusta. I went home to play with Ford at Lone Oak.

But the great Philip Parkin never really made it. He now announces on the Golf Channel. He's the guy with the sweet British accent saying stuff like, "This putt breaks a lot more than the players think."

Lots of people never make it in pro golf. Could be anything. Women, wine, yips, injuries. Talent is not enough.

Philip is proof that golf will ultimately win.

You can take nothing for granted. Tell golf you have figured it out and it will return with a vengeance to destroy you. Ask Philip.

41

- *'FULLY BOOKED, SIR'* -

MUIRFIELD

*For we all must appear
before the judgment
seat of Christ.*
2 Corinthians 5:10

THE FAMOUS MUIRFIELD GOLF CLUB is located in a small town called Gullane.

I love it so much I should probably live there. It is about 30 minutes east of Edinburgh. My first time there was in 1984. I had come to Scotland to try to qualify for the British Open. In those days, it was way too easy for American amateurs to get in. With a scratch handicap, we were exempted into the final qualifier.

"Huh? Are you serious? That's crazy!" When I figured that out, I said, "Why not? Let's go!" So my brother-in-law Steve met me again to caddy and we played two wonderful rounds at Leven Links.

When I failed to qualify—more than predictable—Steve and I drove over to Muirfield to see if there was any possibility to play. Nicklaus had named his course in Ohio "Muirfield Village." This was the real thing, a special place.

The course in Gullane is just the latest home of the Honourable Company of Edinburgh Golfers, a club that can document its continuous existence back to 1744.

That makes it, as far as its members are concerned, the oldest golf club in the world. At least one other Scottish club, the Royal Burgess Golfing Society, claims to be older—but it doesn't have papers to prove it.

The Honourable Company has the papers, and facsimiles of them are on display in glass cases inside the quasi-Tudor clubhouse.

We arrived on a Tuesday afternoon, perhaps around 2 PM. The qualifier at Leven Links was conducted on Sunday and Monday. We planned to stay in Scotland and watch the Open and enjoy some golf. Our secret hope: to play Muirfield that Tuesday.

There were no more than five cars in the car park. No fence kept me out, so I wandered into the most likely place to find some human to provide information.

If there was a "pro shop," I never saw it. I did, however, finally locate the secretary's office.

The place had wooden floors. It was very old. Almost spooky, actually.

Before even seeing anyone, I felt like an intruder in heaven, waiting to be thrown out. There were no "Welcome" signs, but there also were no "Keep Out" signs.

I opened the door to one large room. Lots of file cabinets. Two desks. By the window to our left a middle-aged lady sat behind her desk. She said nothing. She never really looked up, although I think she sneaked a peek to see who the intruder might be.

Another, larger desk was directly in front of us. It was 1984 and therefore there were no computers on the desk. But papers, papers, everywhere papers.

The older gentlemen sitting behind the bigger desk was obviously in charge. He was well-dressed: blue blazer, tie, white shirt. He was also overweight and had too much hair.

There was no nameplate because there was no reason to announce who he was.

He was the famous Major G.J. Vanreenen, secretary for the Honourable Company of Edinburgh Golfers. He had replaced Paddy Hamner, a notorious curmudgeon of a man who was loved for his rudeness. Stories of these guys are legend.

Now let me add my true story of Vanreenen to the legend.

His primary duty was to manage the affairs at the club we all know as Muirfield. His secondary duty was to keep away the riffraff, such as lawyers from Kentucky.

He never looked up. No one acknowledged our presence. Steve followed behind as I led our band of two into enemy territory. Like Joshua and Caleb entering the Promised Land, we were the grasshoppers and they were the giants.

We had decided on a simple strategy. We were hoping it would be easy. Just pay a fee and walk on.

If necessary, I would tell them I was a "competitor" in the Open. If that failed, I would mention that I was a member of the bar. I had heard that several members of Muirfield were advocates and solicitors, my fellow lawyers. I would mention that I was a member in good standing at Lexington Country Club. I would try not to lie, although I would say whatever else would perhaps impress whoever was in charge to let us play a simple round of golf. We would carry our own clubs if no caddies were available. We would be no trouble at all. Just let us play a simple round of golf on a virtually empty golf course. Money was no object.

But now our strategy was in big trouble.

We were obviously in the right place. I had been in Scotland enough to know the secretary controls play of guests.

I was standing five feet away from the man himself, sitting at his desk. He never looked up. He never said a word. He totally ignored me.

A visit with the Wizard of Oz could not have been more intimidating.

I coughed. I shuffled my feet.

Finally, I nervously said, "Good afternoon, Major. My name is Tim Philpot. I am here to qualify for the Open. Unfortunately, I failed to qualify yesterday."

I paused, leaving the false inference that my failure to qualify was a shock, hoping he might mistake me for a real player. He did not need to know that the Lexington City Championship was a "major" for me.

"We hoped perhaps today to be permitted the honor to play your course."

Silence.

He was busy doing something. Too busy to look up. Too busy to speak.

I continued, knowing that I was too close and too desperate to stop. I had come too far to quit now.

"Of course, I play off scratch at Lexington Country Club in Lexington, Kentucky, U.S.A. We of course understand we would be paying a full green fee. We could play any day this week if you have any times available."

The sun was shining. There were five cars in the lot. There were plenty of times "available." At least that is what I was seeing.

The Major seemed to have heard nothing.

I continued: "I am an attorney at law and member of the bar in good standing." Nothing.

"It has been my lifelong dream to play one round of golf at Muirfield, the Honourable Company of Edinburgh Golfers."

Finally the great man spoke.

The Wizard was in full form. He never actually looked up. He continued to write or read or whatever he was doing. But his voice was unmistakable. He spoke, but not to me.

"Mrs. Mustard."

"Yes, sir?"

"Please look at the ledger kindly. Are there any times available?"

Without looking at any notes or records, the answer came loud and clear from Mrs. Mustard's corner of the large room: "Fully booked, sir. We are fully booked."

Only then did the great man look up at Steve and me. His head moved very deliberately and his eyes finally zeroed in on mine. This was not the first time that Vanreenen and Mrs. Mustard had tag-teamed innocent Americans.

Oh my God, I thought to myself. I was so petrified by now that I barely remember what came next, but it was something like this.

Vanreenen delivered a speech about Muirfield and the sanctity of the holy ground upon which we stood. It brought to mind the Old Testament story of Moses standing face to face with God, which is something you are not supposed to do.

"Young man, of course you would like to play here. Everyone wants to play here. Even this morning Jack Nicklaus, Tom Watson and J.C. Snead called and wanted to play. They received the same answer as you. Perhaps you are unaware that this is the finest golf club in the world and our protocol for visitors is well-established. We are fully booked."

He then became just a little more polite and directed Mrs. Mustard to give us information about how to properly book a tee time, since we were obviously two idiots unfamiliar with it.

Later, I often wondered if J.C. Snead knew how great he was to be mentioned in the same breath as Jack Nicklaus and Tom Watson.

But if God and his judgment seat are anything like Major Vanreenen, I'm worried. Worried, but ready.

42

- 'PLEASE, LADIES, DON'T GO' -
THE LADIES OF GULLANE

"I never stopped warning each of you night and day with tears."

Acts 20:31

IN 1984, FORD JOINED ME IN SCOTLAND. No preaching. Just golf.

We attended the British Open at St. Andrews (won by Seve Ballesteros, if you remember). We then played golf with about a dozen men.

We actually played St. Andrews on the Monday after the tournament ended, with the holes still in the same place as Sunday. White paint still lined the holes. I remember being tempted to take some of that paint home. Very cool.

Ford was not too impressed with the Old Course. He couldn't break 80 on it, so he didn't like it. He wondered where the trees were. And the water hazards. He acted like he didn't like it because it was too easy, but in reality he didn't like it because Ford liked places where he could break 80. Or at least 90. I think he shot a generous 93. The Old Course is harder than it looks on TV.

For some reason, he liked Troon, which is so hard that no one really loves it. But I quickly figured out that Dad had made a few putts that day and beat whomever he wanted to beat and, therefore, he liked Troon. He made par on the famous Postage Stamp eighth hole.

Most sane people play match play or Stableford rules in the British Isles.

Why? It is simple. Putting down your real score in medal play is too depressing. For instance, if a golfer with a 16-handicap shot 100, that would be 24 points in a Stableford game and he wouldn't have to feel so bad.

One hundred sounds bad. And is. Twenty-four points doesn't sound so bad, even if it is. Dad would have loved Stableford rules if he could have figured it out: One point for a bogey, two points for a par, three points for a birdie, four points for an eagle. All net. Way too complicated for Ford.

BUT THE BIGGEST MEMORY of Ford in Scotland was at Gullane.

You'll recall that Major Vanreenen had made sure we were not playing Muirfield. So we had settled for the next best thing, Gullane No. 1.

Gullane Golf Club has three courses, each assigned a number. It's simple. There is no "Valley Course," or "Mountain Course," or "Old Course." Just One, Two or Three.

When you get high atop the seventh tee on the No. 1 Course, you can see forever across the Firth of Forth, and see Muirfield sitting down below in the valley.

The view makes you want to camp there and stay awhile.

But on the day we played, it was drizzling when we teed off, and by the time Ford reached the third tee, atop a giant hill, the drizzle had become a downpour and nothing the caddies could say would change Ford's opinion that it was time to walk in while there was still hope. The course goes out and never comes back until the eighteenth hole.

It was now or never to get back alive.

Ford's playing partners, including me, totally agreed.

We made it back with the wind blowing 30 miles an hour, with our umbrellas upside down and our bodies totally drenched to the bone. And it was cold, even for July.

As we got back, Ford was shocked to see two ladies on the first tee, hitting a tee shot and heading out into that same wind and cold rain. They were old women. Older than Ford, who was 67.

Being a man of God, he felt it was his duty to go speak to these lost souls and explain that perhaps they had not noticed, but it was raining cold drops on winds from hell. Just as he would speak to a drunk about his drinking, he pleaded with these two members of the Ladies Golf Association, who had a competition scheduled, that to continue down that first fairway would be a journey into golf oblivion. Disaster awaited if they continued.

He told them, "It is raining here, but up on that hill on the third hole it is raining and blowing so hard you can't stand up. Please ladies, don't go."

One of the ladies, who could have been old Tom Morris' second wife, looked straight at Ford and said, "Thank you, sir, but we must play a round of golf today. If we waited for good weather in Gullane, we would never play."

I must admit, she was right about that.

And off the ladies went, with the unsuccessful evangelist left behind to mutter and bemoan the sure fate of these two lost souls.

When Ford made it into the bar area to dry off and get some hot tea, all he could talk about was the two crazy women he met on the first tee. He spoke with passion about trying to save their souls.

In the end, Ford and Scotland were not the perfect match. He didn't get to show off his good tan.

43

'FINE, SIR. EVERYTHING IS FINE' -

DOUGLAS

*The boy looked so much like
a corpse that many said,
"He's dead."*
Mark 9:26

HEATHER WAS THE ONLY FEMALE CADDIE at Gullane. When my brother-in-law Steve Davis and I went there for a routine round of golf in 1983, we arrived at a time when the regular caddies were somehow not available.

So Heather was called, and with real caddies not around, her son Douglas was also enlisted to caddy for these two poor Americans.

As my life has unfolded, Douglas is one of my most vivid golf memories. He was smaller than my bag. He wanted very much to caddy, but there was serious doubt that he could physically do it.

My bag was big. I was in Scotland to play in the British Amateur, so I had a big bag worthy of such a participant.

Gullane's second hole goes straight uphill. It's less than 400 yards but so extremely uphill you can barely get there in two good shots.

Douglas was dragging along, many yards behind, struggling to carry that behemoth bag. I was seriously worried that I might be killing the kid. He got to the second green, threw down the bag, and gasped.

I asked, "Douglas, are you OK?" His countenance immediately changed from pain to a smile as he looked up at me and said, "Fine, sir. Everything is fine."

Several times throughout the day I asked Douglas if he was OK. The answer was always the same. "Fine sir. Everything is fine."

When I returned home, I realized I had found my illustration for life. What a great picture of how business and professional people fake it all day, every day. We spend the day telling people we are fine when in fact we are usually quite *not*-fine.

Financial issues and marriage problems.

Children in crisis and work emergencies.

In fact, the first step to God is to admit that we are not "fine." We have a long way to go from fine. But we keep playing the game hoping no one will find out.

Actually, golf is good for you because the game will expose you. There is a scorecard. No way to say you played good but shot 108.

Ask a golfer how he's playing and the answer will never be "fine."

There is no way to say, as in basketball, that even though you were not shooting well you played good defense. No such thing.

A number at the end of the card tells us everything we want to know. No excuses. It is what it is.

A number. A number that defines your day.

In fact, a handicap index, if honest, is a number that defines who you are as a golfer. Who am I? According to GHIN, right now I am a 3.7 and trending upward. That's who I am.

I am not fine.

I'm a 3.7.

44

- WESTERN GAILES -
DONALD

*"It is not good for man to be
alone. I will make a helper
suitable for him."*
Genesis 2:18

M Y CADDIE AT WESTERN GAILES was Donald Fox.
His father was the caddie master. I arrived for British
Open qualifying in 1987 so early that I got the best caddie
available, which was Donald. Western Gailes is a wonderful
course near Irvine on the western coast of Scotland.

Donald grew up there. He slept at the course many nights
in a drunken stupor. He was in his 20s but already had been
to prison, I was told. He went to an Irvine bar every night, and
when the bar closed at 2 AM he hopped the train for Glasgow
where the bars stayed open until 4 AM.

But he was on the first tee at whatever time he was needed,
whether 7 AM or 1 PM.

Time made no difference to Donald. He would sleep on
the train back from Glasgow and head straight to the first tee
if needed. He only needed enough money to drink. This kept
his expenses down.

I still remember in my first practice round that I had 170
yards downwind to the pin, a blind shot over a mound to a

small green on the front side somewhere. Donald handed me a sand wedge and told me to aim 30 yards right of the flag, which I could barely see over the hill. I argued.

But he said, "Just trust me, laddie."

I followed his advice and of course the ball trickled down a ramp he knew about and rolled up to 10 feet from the hole. I never questioned him again.

He knew Western Gailes like Adam knew Eve.

He was a far better caddie than I was a golfer. As Bagger Vance said when asked if he was a caddie, "Don't know. You a golfer?"

FOR SOME STRANGE REASON, Donald has been on my heart now for 25 years. I think the reason is that he was the best caddie at Western Gailes, and I was probably the worst player trying to qualify for the Open. He didn't care. As long as I paid him what we had agreed on, he was fine.

I kept waiting for him to dump me for a European Tour player needing a caddie. Someone who might actually make it. He must have figured out in our practice rounds that I was not Open caliber. I knew it. Surely he did. When he gently inquired about what tournaments I had won, I don't think he was too impressed that I was the reigning Lone Oak Invitational Champion. I don't think my Campbellsville Country Club Invitational championship gave much hope that I was a "player" either.

But he stuck with me and encouraged me. He helped me. I even played pretty well. There were a couple of moments when it looked like I might sneak into the Open, the way a hungry man sneaks into the kitchen after the lights are out, hoping no one finds out who's in there.

And the story continues into 2010. I went back to Western Gailes to play. I asked for Donald at the caddie shack. I could not remember his last name.

"Donald Fox?"

"Yes, that's him. Donald Fox. His father was the caddie master."

"He's on the course. Can I tell him who's looking for him?"

"Tim Philpot. He won't remember me. I played in an Open qualifier in 1987. He was my caddie."

"I'll tell him to wait on you when he gets in."

In fact, the weather was horrible that day. All caddies were out on the course. So I carried my own clubs and played 18 holes by myself in the rain. And when it was over, I went to find Donald in the caddie shack. He stepped out. I looked at him and he looked at me. He sort of looked the same but not really.

"Donald?"

"No, I'm Donald's brother."

"Oh, well that makes sense."

We exchanged warm greetings and he told me he well remembered me. Lying probably. He told me he was not sure where Donald was now. He finally confessed he had not seen Donald in a quite a while. He ran off a few months ago and was now drinking too much and had a boyfriend.

Ouch. I didn't see that one coming.

All the more reason to pray for Donald and hope to see him again someday.

But maybe his brother did remember me, since my name is forever on the clubhouse wall at Western Gailes. Not because I was a great golfer, but because I could read and write.

In the Open qualifier I kept score for a kid who broke the amateur course record that day with a 66. I looked for the framed scorecard which I had seen on many future trips to the old course. I "attested" the score which stood on the wall at Western Gailes for more than 20 years.

My highest moment in golf was keeping score for someone you never heard of and whose name is now forgotten.

45

- 'YOU A CADDIE?' -

PERFECT GOLF

So we say with confidence,
"The Lord is my helper;
I will not be afraid."
Hebrews 13:6

D OUGLAS AND DONALD and their colleagues of all times and places raise the whole issue of caddies in general and how one should play golf.

There are five basic versions of golf.

1. Walk and carry your own clubs.

This has obvious drawbacks. Walking eighteen holes is a six-mile adventure. The walk itself is plenty for most people, but to then carry 25 pounds strapped over your shoulder is sheer misery. Especially if you are 60 years old.

2. Walk with a pull cart (a "trolley" in Europe).

This too is a weak system, especially when you don't hit it in the fairway. There is nothing worse than your trolley turning over when you try to take it over a hill or sidehill lie. Walking is nice. But fighting with that pull cart in the rough is almost harder than just carrying a nice light bag.

3. Ride in a cart (a "buggy" in Europe).

This seems to be the perfect solution, but the truth is that walking is how golf was meant to be played. It's just not right. Riding around was unthinkable to our founding fathers of golf.

With carts, it is "stop and go." Sit down. Stand up. Left. Right. Feels like a Catholic church. Up. Down. In the cart. Back out of the cart.

Golf was intended to be played from your ball, straight from one shot to the next. This cannot happen in carts.

4. "Cart path only."

This is the worst by far. If there is golf in hell, it will be "cart path only."

Sideways all day. The cart has to stay on the path, which means if the cart path is left, slicers are all day taking four clubs and walking sideways to the other side hoping to find the ball and hit it the right distance with one of the four clubs.

This is truly a miserable experience.

When you get there with your four clubs, usually you discover that none of the clubs you brought is the right one. You hit it bad, then walk sideways back to the cart path, 50 yards away, trying to figure out what to do now. Five-hour rounds are routine. Six hours is possible.

5. Perfect golf.

Walk. Five miles. Eighteen holes. With a caddie. A real one. Not just a bag carrier, although that's not bad either. He (or she):

> carries your burdens for you,
> whispers truth in your ear,
> encourages you,

provides useful information,
pats you on the back,
asks you to reevaluate questionable decisions,
and keeps you moving straight ahead,
all for a measly $20-$60.
Wow!

Golf was even a two-man game hundreds of years ago.

A player could not play golf without a caddie out there in the heather and tall grasses. The second man was needed to find the ball and lead the way toward the hole. Golf was a team sport in the beginning. The two-person "teams" in the links lands of Scotland were the essence of the game. One guy hits the ball and the other leads the way to the hole. I like that.

Just watch the guys on TV with their caddies and tell me that this is not perfect golf. They walk... but slowly. They talk... and smile. They sweat... but not from hard work.

In fact, the only thing better than being a player might be to be a caddie.

You are involved with the game and get all the benefits of being on the course with the wind and green grass and God's beautiful nature and exercise without the pain of missing any three-footers.

Perfect golf. Ford would have agreed.

46

- MY MISSIONARY CADDIE -

BILLY DAVIS

*So Moses went out to meet
his father-in-law and bowed
down and kissed him.*
Exodus 18:7

O NE OF THE BIG THRILLS of my meager career was qualifying for the U.S. Mid-Amateur in 1988. It was special because my caddie was Billy Davis, my father-in-law. His son Steve was my caddie in Scotland for the British Am. Those Davis boys made good caddies.

Billy was also Ford's best friend on earth.

Billy came home for good from 25 missionary years in Africa in about 1980. He took up golf. Way too late to be good, but he loved it. He would go play a lousy par-3 course by himself and have more fun than most guys would have at Augusta playing with Bobby Jones.

Billy was a man of adventure, which helps when you don't hit many greens or fairways. He moved a wife and four kids to Africa in the early 1950s when it took a boat several weeks to get there. He could preach in four languages. He hunted every type of big game known to man. Hippo, cape buffalo, antelope of all kinds. You name it, he killed it.

And at the end of his tenure, he did the unthinkable. He

flew his Cessna 180—the smallest plane you can imagine—from Congo to Kentucky. Up through Africa to Egypt to Switzerland to Scotland to Iceland to Nova Scotia to Kentucky. Without real instruments.

He was a real man and the perfect best friend for Ford.

Billy and I drove from Kentucky to Kansas City, stopped to watch the Royals play baseball, had a flat tire in Lawrence, Kansas, and finally made it to Prairie Dunes, a famous course in the middle of nowhere.

If you miss the fairway at Prairie Dunes, you look for your ball in waist-high grass. Perfect for Billy, the big game hunter from Africa.

On one of my nines, I well remember making six pars and still shooting 44 (nine over par), with three drives into oblivion resulting in three triple bogies.

He was a great hunter in the wilds of Africa, but not even Billy could find my hooks and slices in the Prairie Dunes rough.

I missed the cut and came home, but what an experience to be with my missionary father-in-law for those few days.

Bad golf on a great course with the right people is better than good golf on a mediocre course with the wrong ones.

Billy got Alzheimer's in his later years, and when he passed away he was not the same man who flew home from Africa to Kentucky or preached in four languages. But he was still special.

My last memories of him are of a simple old man singing hymns to himself.

Smiling. Loving.

He was in another world that included Jesus Himself.

This world, as great as it is, is not our home.

47

- BEST FRIENDS -

FORD AND BILLY

*And Jonathan had David
reaffirm his oath...because he
loved him as he loved himself.*
1 Samuel 20:17

FORD AND BILLY DAVIS were such close friends that it would not be too wrong to say that they arranged my marriage to Susan Angelina Davis. Billy's daughter and Ford's son just happened to be four months apart.

Sue and I were too young to know what was happening, but these preacher buds were probably happily conniving behind the scenes to get their kids to fall in love.

In fact, I did not just fall in love with Sue. I fell in love with her whole family.

If you have to have a mother-in-law, Doris seemed like a great option.

Sue's brothers Steve and Mark were super athletes and great older brother figures.

Her sister Lindy was five years younger and made a cute little sister.

I liked everything about this Davis family.

Sue was gorgeous and had a great family. What more can you ask for?

And the same friendship between Ford and Billy continued forever. Some of my most pleasant memories of them came from watching those two old guys sitting in the eighth row at Rupp Arena rooting on the Kentucky Wildcats.

They had to peer through the cheerleaders to see the game. I think I know why they were having fun!

They complained about every call from the blind referees.

Wondered why the coach did such a stupid thing.

Ford and Billy were more fun to watch than the game.

48

- 'MINNIEFIELD, YOU DRIBBLE TOO MUCH!' -
'CATS

Their land is full of idols.
Isaiah 2:8

FORD WAS A BASKETBALL REFEREE in the 1940s and 50s. He would often help the famous Adolph Rupp by refereeing basketball practices for his University of Kentucky Wildcats. He worked high school and small college games almost every night. In his drinking days, he would often referee somewhere on Friday night and not find his way home until Saturday morning or even Saturday night. Virginia was not happy.

She was a saint, but not a happy one.

In 1972 Joe B. Hall was granted the impossible job of following Coach Rupp. Kentucky basketball is a form of idol worship in the state of Kentucky. This means the coach is highly scrutinized. Hall's job was always in jeopardy, since he was not Rupp himself. Fans were hard to please until he finally won the NCAA championship in 1978. Even then, he was whispered about.

Except by Ford.

He loved Joe B. because the coach would invite Ford to "speak" to the team at least twice a year. The idea was for Ford

153

to give a motivational speech with as much Gospel as he could muster on that day.

Ford contended until the day he died that he was personally responsible for the great win at the finals of the SEC tournament in Nashville one year when the Wildcats held off Auburn and Charles Barkley.

Ford's speech and prayer made the difference.

Forget that Vegas had Kentucky as a solid six-point favorite.

And of course he never mentioned the time they lost to LSU in the NCAA Tournament after one of those Ford speeches. He was strangely silent following that debacle.

I ONLY WENT WITH HIM ONCE. We went to Memorial Coliseum for one of the Ford motivational speeches. But after that, I was so worried about what he would say that I never went back.

My brother Danny went another time (and I am glad I missed it), when Ford, instead of providing spiritual motivation and encouragement, decided to turn basketball coach instead. Joe B. must have been appalled, and in fact this may have been Ford's last basketball sermon.

He looked straight at Dirk Minniefield, the UK point guard and later first-round pick in the NBA draft, and said: "Minniefield, you dribble the ball too much. Quit walking up the floor," demonstrating with his hands how it was not to be done.

"Get rid of that ball... run with it!"

Just what Joe B. needed. Another preacher who thought he was a coach.

49

- 'LORD, I REALLY NEED THIS PUTT' -

PRAYER

And pray in the Spirit on all occasions with all kinds of prayers and requests.

Ephesians 6:18

JUST AS THERE ARE NO ATHEISTS IN FOXHOLES, there are very few on the golf course.

The name of Jesus is often mentioned in golf and not usually with "Praise" as His first name. He even has middle initials at some golf courses. It usually follows a missed putt, especially lipouts. Or when a bad bounce sends a ball into a hazard or out of bounds.

As I often think when I hear that, *You're calling on the Creator of the universe and the all-knowing, all-powerful God a little late, aren't you? Don't you think it might make more sense to talk to Him* before *you hit the shot instead of* after?

Who is there among us who has not thought something like this: *Lord, you know I would love to make this four-foot putt.* It is not really a prayer, per se. No one wants to admit they actually ask God to intervene in golf. It is far too trivial. Earthquakes and tornadoes and death and disease are worthy of real prayer, but not four-footers.

Imagine your typical Sunday school class. "Any prayer requests?"

"Yes, my Aunt Dorothy is having surgery next Tuesday. Uncle John's cancer has come back. My friend Joey is still on drugs. My cousin Sally is going through a tough divorce. We don't want to forget to pray for the folks who just went through the floods in Missouri and the tornadoes in Alabama. And of course the war in Afghanistan. Let's don't forget the boys in uniform.

"And (drumroll)… I am playing next week in the Club Championship. Pray for my nerves and good putting stroke. I really need to hit at least 10 fairways and 12 greens to have a chance. I get a lesson tomorrow, so ask the Lord to give my teacher all the right words and give me the ability to hear him."

But even if that imaginary scenario makes us realize some sober truth about this game we love, it doesn't mean we don't pray on the course. It is human nature to ask for some divine help for such a difficult game.

I have not promised to go be a missionary in Africa if God would help me break par today, but that's not too far off.

And one of my absolute best memories of Ford is praying on a course.

I was probably 35 years old, playing with Ford in Florida one day. One of his good friends Barry Bertram missed the Florida trip due to cancer surgery. On about the twelfth hole, Dad remembered that his friend Barry had surgery that morning and he openly confessed that he had forgotten to pray for his friend.

He hit his second shot from the fairway. He then got down on his knees in the middle of the fairway and prayed out loud for Barry. Just perhaps a minute or so. But very loud. Very visible.

And he didn't see the guys behind us wondering what was taking so long up there. I was sort of miffed that Ford would hold up the golf course to pray for Barry.

But here I am, 30 years later, with a memory that will never go away.

I learned it is never too late to pray.

It is OK to forget to pray.

It is OK to pray when you do remember.

And it is OK to pray on a golf course.

In the middle of the day. In the middle of the twelfth fairway.

PERHAPS THAT DAY IS WHAT GAVE ME the courage to pray for a new friend named Tom Pope. It was some sort of member-member event at my club. I did not know Tom. He was a nice guy and a good player but did a couple of odd things during the round that made us all look at each other. Like pick his ball up before he finished the hole. You know that feeling. This is a real tournament, and this guy did not finish the hole. *What do I put down for him?*

He knew he wasn't right, and said, "Hey, guys. Sorry about today. My wife has cancer and we've had a bad week. My mind is not here today." Or something like that.

We all said, "Sorry, man." Or something like that.

We finished on the fourteenth hole (it was a shotgun start). And as we finished and got ready to head back in, I found myself saying to Tom and the others: "Guys, would it be all right if we prayed right here, right now for Tom and his wife?"

We stood on the fourteenth green and held hands and prayed for Tom and his wife, who died a few weeks later. As you might imagine, Tom and I are now friends.

I learned that from Ford. It's never too late to pray. And it's never too soon to pray. And it's OK to pray on the fourteenth green.

PERHAPS THE GREATEST LESSON I ever learned on prayer came from an unknown, thin young man in Ethiopia. I was there supposedly to speak but instead was spoken to.

I don't even think he knew what he was saying, but I cannot forget it:

> "There will likely be lots of preachers in hell.
> But there will be no men of prayer in hell."

Wow! He hit the essence of it.

The reality of who we are is not found in what we appear to be on a stage in front of thousands of people. The reality is found in the quietness of our hearts and prayer closets, seeking the heart and will of God for others and ourselves.

I have not made it yet. But I'd rather be a man of prayer than a man of the pulpit. And as a postscript, 25 years later Barry Bertram is alive and well.

Ford's prayers mattered.

50

- 'I NEED A TENT' -

GETTING OLD

*They will still bear fruit
in old age.*
Psalm 92:14

FORD HATED GETTING OLD. His vision of himself was handsome, with black wavy hair, shirtless—the Marine picture with a cigarette hanging out of his mouth, even though he preached against cigarettes. He was a man who needed to be seen.

That probably explains why in 1959 he started the first real religious TV show in America, *The Story*.

I can still hear the professional announcer say, "And now, *The Story*… with your host, Ford Philpot."

Google it sometime. You'll be impressed. It's part of history. That era of the late 50s and early 60s was all about Red Skelton, *Howdy Doody*, *The Lone Ranger*, *Gunsmoke*, *Bonanza*, Alfred Hitchcock, Walter Cronkite, Huntley and Brinkley, *I Love Lucy*, and—if you look deep enough—Ford Philpot.

TV preachers were not yet a dirty word. And since he loved the latest technology in preaching just as much as he did in golf, Ford knew just what to do when the cameras started rolling.

Ford simply wanted to let the world in on the story of Jesus and his love. And, of course, he liked to look good telling that story.

So when he was about 70, and preaching to small crowds in small churches instead of thousands of people on TV or stadiums, he was not happy. He longed for the good old days. He even told me in about 1990 that he thought he needed to get a tent. He was remembering the 1950s when he had a tent that seated 1,000 people. He was sure it would work again. I told him that, sadly, the days of tent revivals were over. He knew it was true, but he didn't like it.

There is no Senior Tour for tournament preachers.

He looked in the mirror and did not see the handsome young basketball star who swayed the girls. Or the wavy-haired soldier who impressed his buddies. Or the preacher who brought thousands into the Kingdom of God.

His phone was not ringing off the hook. He was not turning down invitations anymore. He had no private airplane to get him from one town to the next because he was so busy. The letters and cards had stopped coming in. He was actually accepting offers to go preach in prisons, where getting a crowd together was easy.

And of course golf was the ultimate revealer. Golf told him for sure that he was getting older.

He couldn't break 90 anymore.

He needed a wood for his second shot too often.

The yellow pants didn't look good on him.

The 7-iron stayed in the bag.

He could not hit it over the green anymore.

51

- 'I TOLD YOU I WAS SICK' -

DEATH

Who can live and not see
death, or who can escape
the power of the grave?
Psalm 89:48

IN 1992, FORD HAD A HEART ATTACK. It was not all bad news.

As a raging hypochondriac, he was almost proud of the confirmation that indeed it was a real heart attack.

Open heart surgery in 1978 had been a wonderful experience for him. His second open heart surgery nine years later was even better.

Hypochondriacs love to say, "I told you so." As he said so well: "I tried to tell you all I was sick."

The last conversation I had with him on this earth was about golf.

I say "on this earth" because I go to his grave on occasion and we talk. That's another issue.

Dad had congestive heart failure. He was weak. We didn't really know he would die within hours, but we knew it was bad.

It was a Sunday evening in the hospital room, on March 9, 1992. He was very uncomfortable, but the PGA Tour was playing at Doral, where Raymond Floyd won. I remember because we often discussed Raymond and how well he chipped and putted.

I asked him if he had been able to watch the golf tournament Sunday afternoon and he shook his head "no."

That meant that he was really sick this time. He always watched Sunday afternoon golf.

We talked as I sat at his bedside. His eyes were closed for most of the conversation.

"Hey, Dad, Raymond Floyd won at Doral today."

He smiled.

"Remember that day we played Doral with Alvin Dark?"

He smiled again and nodded. Of course he remembered Alvin Dark. He was a Major League Baseball All-Star. He had been manager of the San Francisco Giants. In college playing football, he was a star back for LSU and Southwestern Louisiana. Ford knew him because he had heard that Alvin was a Jesus follower and called him to come give his testimony at a Ford Philpot Crusade. He was not afraid to call anyone.

George Foreman went to Africa with Dad in 1979 and shared his new-found faith in the same stadium where Muhammad Ali whooped him a few years earlier. Ford loved to be with famous people.

"As I remember, Alvin was a pretty good player."

Ford nodded agreement. Alvin was a scratch golfer on top of being a great ballplayer.

"I really like Raymond. He made some putts today."

Dad nodded agreement. He also really liked Raymond. For one thing, Raymond was an older player. For another, he well remembered that day in Dayton, Ohio, in 1969, when we went to the PGA Championship together.

Raymond Floyd had style. He walked with a strut. Ford also liked to strut, whether it was when someone recognized him for being a "famous" preacher, or when someone called him "Doc" so he could pretend for just a moment to be a real doctor, or just from making a 20-foot putt to beat Uncle Jule on the eighteenth green. He had a cocky strut, even at times when he had nothing to strut about.

Raymond probably hit it over the greens. Like a real man.

I said good night and told him, "I'll be back tomorrow." There was no "I love you" or other such mushy talk. We didn't talk that way directly to each other. He didn't know how. I understood then and I understand now.

I left to go home since I was expected on the floor of the Kentucky State Senate the next morning. My wife Sue kept watch with dad.

She came home in the middle of the night and the phone rang soon thereafter. Dad was not going to make it. We dressed and headed to the hospital, picking up my mom on the way.

To understand what happened next, you must understand that dad had two pet peeves about other preachers.

One was liberals. He could not understand how anyone could be a liberal. He was not sure what that meant, but he had no use for them. In general, it meant clergy persons who might not believe everyone needs to "get saved" like he did. They might not believe in hell like he did. They might wear a white collar instead of the nice suit like he did. They might still take a drink instead of quitting like he did. They might preach for 20 minutes and not say much. They might not sweat when they preach. They might not play golf like he did. If they did, they were slicers.

And second, fat people in general were the punchline on many a Ford joke. Especially fat preachers. So, with that in mind...

THE DOCTOR CAME INTO THE WAITING ROOM to tell us that Dad had passed away. And who should follow moments later but the hospital chaplain.

He was fat.

He was "liberal," or at least that would be our presumption based on his nametag's denominational affiliation.

He offered to take us back to say goodbye. We stood around Ford's body. This fat and liberal preacher prayed a beautiful and profound prayer over the body of my dad. I smiled and maybe even laughed out loud.

I could almost hear Ford and God conversing. God was explaining that fat people and liberals were also useful in the Kingdom of God.

Ford was suddenly understanding concepts he had never even considered!

My guess is that Ford also asked who won at Doral, just to be sure.

He probably wanted to know if Jack Nicklaus at 52 was too old to win another major.

With lots of daylight and a new body, no telling how many holes he plays in heaven every day before being sent off to some planet to preach at night.

That would be heaven for Ford.

I know this sounds almost heretical, but hopefully there are some sinners in need of a Savior even in the heavens. Ford's job was to preach the good news and save sinners.

I hope the Lord has sent him on a preaching mission somewhere with a golf course.

52

- AT LEAST ONE ANGEL -

RAYMOND'S EPILOGUE

"...there is rejoicing in the presence of the angels of God over one sinner who repents."
Luke 15:10

Now, 20 YEARS LATER, there is more to the story of Ford's death and Raymond Floyd.

In March 2011, a friend in California, Steve Garrison, told me that he had been to a Champions Tour banquet on a Tuesday night near Newport Beach. PGA and U.S. Open Champion Larry Nelson shared an incredible story of Raymond Floyd's recent experience of praying to trust in Christ over the previous two weeks. Apparently, his wife had cancer and Champions Tour chaplain Tom Randall went to Houston to pray with her and Raymond.

It was really exciting for me because I can honestly say I have prayed for Raymond—not often, but when I would think about it.

I prayed for him because I always loved his style on the golf course. And I prayed for him because he was in the middle of the last conversation I ever had with Dad on earth.

You remember stuff like that.

I loved to hear Raymond talk about the game of golf.

I loved him because he was a world-class golfer with a lousy swing that no one would ever try to copy.

I loved it when he would take out the pin for a chip shot and then hole it like he knew he would.

I loved it when he let his caddie take the ball out of the hole and he just turned and walked to the next tee, because he was way too cool to have to reach down and pick a ball out of the hole.

I loved him because I had seen him kiss his adult son after a golf game on one of those made-for-TV golf events. I don't know this, but I suspect he tells his sons he loves them. I hope so.

I loved him because he won the first tour event I ever attended, the PGA Championship at the NCR Club in Dayton, Ohio, in 1969.

A very young Raymond Floyd—about 26 or so—won that 1969 PGA for his first major and beat all my heroes, so I decided he was a cool guy.

I loved stories about him. I think I remember him accurately declaring after the U.S. Open at Shinnecock, which he won at age age 42, that he deliberately hit his ball in a front bunker because he knew he couldn't stop the ball below the hole on the green from his lie. His only hope for par or birdie was to hole the bunker shot. He knew he would never get it up and down from over the green or even two-putt from above the hole.

And then he holed it.

If that's true, I love it.

If not, it ought to be.

Even his name. He does not go by "Ray." He is Raymond. The full name. And everyone knows who that is. "Everybody loves Raymond."

ALL OF THAT IS TO SAY I exclaimed "Wow!" really loud when I heard Raymond's new story of salvation. I could hear the angels in heaven rejoicing over his new life in Christ. And that caused me to remember that my last conversation with my dad was about Raymond Floyd.

I told Steve a shorter version of the story about Raymond and my dad on his deathbed.

Steve then asked me when dad died. I told him 1992, and I almost fell to the ground when I was reminded that my dad died on March 9, the very same day our conversation was happening!

That day was the nineteenth anniversary of my dad's death and I had not remembered it all day.

I was able to remember my father in a new and sweet way, and that golf was the door for us to have relationship.

And now I was thinking that one of those rejoicing in heaven about Raymond Floyd's salvation was Ford Philpot, my dad.

What a picture! Ford leading the cheers for Raymond's entry into the Kingdom of Heaven.

If that's true, I love it.

If not, it ought to be.

53

- 'I PRAY YOUR LIFE
WILL ALWAYS COUNT' -

NINETEENTH HOLE

Sing to him,
sing praise to him;
tell of all his wonderful acts.
Psalm 105:2

PEOPLE TALK ABOUT LEGACY SOMETIMES.

In fact, if you Google the words *legacy* and *golf*, dozens of courses appear, from Las Vegas to Pinehurst and all sorts of places in between. *Legacy* is quite a popular name for a golf course. Not sure why.

I also know my dad well enough to know for sure that he never once thought about what kind of legacy he would leave behind. That is usually for people who are arrogant enough to believe that they should never be forgotten.

Ford certainly had an arrogant side, sort of cocky, but at the same time he was also humble enough to know that only God would be in charge of what he left behind. He made very little provision for the future of his ministry or his reputation.

He was too busy with the worries of the day, which for him was still saving souls and telling the Good News of Jesus. And an occasional round of golf, still hoping to break 80 when 93 would be a good score.

I do have a special picture, recently found by my brother in his garage. It is a picture of Ford in about 1964, in his preaching heyday, in a basketball arena in Ft. Wayne, Indiana. He was standing before ten thousand empty seats that would be full later that night. It was a great symbol of what he did and who he was—a preacher. Simple. A preacher.

And he signed it. "Dear Tim, I pray that your life will always count for Christ. Love, Dad."

I had the wonderful privilege to be one of only two people who could say to Ford: "Dad."

So I am left with this thought.

His primary legacy is me. And my brother Danny.

We need to learn from his humanness and do better than he did in some areas.

We need to be bold enough and strong enough to be more like Ford in many other areas.

Like meeting no strangers.

Like hating three-putts but loving golf anyway.

Like hitting it right to left, like a real man.

Like sharing your testimony more often.

Like telling people that alcohol will probably kill you.

Like letting people know that a Mulligan (capital M) is available.

Like praying in the middle of a fairway.

Like taking on Jesus to be your caddie.

Ford's world was wonderful.

And it still is.

To Jim and Wally:
Heroes are hard to find sometimes

*And the things you have heard from me in the
presence of many witnesses, entrust to faithful men
who will be able to teach others also.
2 Timothy 2:2*

I AM NOW 61 YEARS OLD and finally appreciating the huge influence of my father. On the world. On our city. On our family. But most personally, on me.

Fatherhood is a huge issue. The federal government is now spending hundreds of millions of dollars to try to fix the problem of missing and abusive fathers. As a judge in Family Court, I see every day the results of no fathers or bad fathers. And on occasion, I see the positive results of a great dad.

In court, I find myself often saying to myself, "I'm starting to really appreciate my parents," after hearing some horror story of fatherhood.

In short, this book is about the fact that my dad showed me it was OK to love both God and golf. But he was not alone.

Other men also showed me the way. Other than my dad, the men who first showed me it was OK to love both Jesus and golf were Jim Hiskey and Wally Armstrong.

They both played on the PGA Tour and were college stars. They started the Links Letter, a newsletter that chronicled God at work on the PGA Tour. They played golf way better than me.

I was barely 30 when I found them—and what a thrill to

see two men who loved God and golf so much!

I cannot write this without thanking them for being an inspiration.

For starters, they both love to write. Wally has written several books, starting with *In His Grip* and more lately including *The Mulligan* with Ken Blanchard. He tried to give me some credit for the thought but that was extremely gracious, because I must have stolen it from someone else who really deserves the credit. Or even better, the Holy Spirit.

Jim still writes a lot for the Links Daily Devotional. His words are always worth reading (www.linksplayers.com).

Wally and I travelled to Australia for two weeks in 2000. We were a good combination. He loved on people and taught golf, and I shared the gospel message of both Jesus and Ol' Tom Morris. Golf and God really are connected. I am sorry for those who don't understand that.

Wally teaches people to swing a golf club in his famous "circle." He also teaches people now about the "chair." He imagines Jesus sitting in a chair every morning, and Wally talks to Him like He is a real person. That is because He is a real person!

After Wally explained what he does (he has just published a book about that experience called, *Practicing the Presence of Jesus*), I have played more golf by myself. I imagine Jesus as a passenger in my cart. We talk. He counsels me. He is my imaginary caddie, except He doesn't have to carry my clubs. I keep an empty chair at most meetings, just so I can remember He is there.

Jim and I also have travelled some, especially to Scotland in the 1980s and again in 2010. I still remember the unforgettable moment when he hooked it off the first tee at St. Andrews so far on a hot dry day that the ball rolled and rolled and rolled until it finally went out of bounds on the road beside the eighteenth hole. Hard to do when the fairway is a hundred yards wide! It was surely the worst shot of his career for an NCAA champion and tour player.

Sue and I will never forget just sitting with Jim in 2010 in the Old Course hotel, eavesdropping for over an hour as he and Bill Rogers, a former British Open champion, talked golf and the universe with Michael Bannon, who taught Rory McIlroy to play golf. Bannon was full of wisdom on how to teach kids the great game of golf.

Just hanging on the fringes of Jim's life brings life to me.

When your dad is a semi-famous mass evangelist, you grow up thinking that the way to make a difference is with "big" meetings with thousands of people.

Jim is one of the main people who showed me that the best meetings have about three or four people. And many of those meetings are at country club bars or patios. He has been changing the world one man at a time.

One conversation at a time.

I learned too late what John Wesley said: "One close conversation is better than ten thousand sermons."

Too bad John Wesley never met a niblick.

Ford may not have agreed with Wesley, because he was sure that if anyone just heard him preach they would find salvation. But there is great truth in Wesley's statement, and Jim Hiskey has proved the value of that statement.

We influence people without even knowing it or trying to be an influence. Wally and Jim were a huge inspiration to me and probably never knew it.

Now they know.

- ACKNOWLEDGEMENTS -

Thanks are in order to two special people. Since I am not a "writer," I needed some professional eyes to help with this project. Pete Bronson and Jeff Hopper helped edit and put the finishing touches on this book. This could not have happened without their friendship and personal love of both golf and Christ, which compelled them to help. Ford would have loved playing golf with both of them. Thanks to Pete and Jeff.

**Expanded photographs and author's notes at
www.fordswonderfulworld.com.**